# WHERE GOD
# MAY BE FOUND

L. Patrick Carroll, S.J.

PAULIST PRESS

New York and Mahwah, N.J.

## DEDICATION

To Edith, my second mother, in her 80th year.
I write this largely in her presence, with her help, and filled with enormous gratitude for the gift of God she is in my life.

## ACKNOWLEDGMENTS

I appreciate enormously the hospitality of Murray residence, a Jesuit Community in Oakland, California, with whom I stayed while I wrote this material.

I am also deeply grateful to staff and friends at St. Leo, many of whom helped me edit this manuscript, and all of whom provided the support for me to be away to write it, as well as much of the story content contained here.

Biblical citations are taken, generally, from *The Catholic Study Bible* (Oxford University Press, 1990), New American Bible, trans., though often the efforts to be inclusive in language are my own rendition.

Copyright © 1994 by the Oregon Province of the Society of Jesus

Library of Congress Cataloging-in-Publication Data

Carroll, L. Patrick, 1936-
    Where God may be found / L. Patrick Carroll.
        p.    cm.
    ISBN 0-8091-3472-1 (paper)
    1. Christian life—Catholic authors. 2. Presence of God. 3. Spiritual exercises. I. Title.
BX2350.2C339    1994
248.4'82—dc20                                                93-48993
                                                                 CIP

Published by Paulist Press
997 Macarthur Blvd.
Mahwah, N.J. 07430

Printed and bound in the United States of America

# Contents

*Seek God, where God may be found ,*
*Call God, while God is near...*
*For just as from the heavens*
*the rain and snow come down*
*And do not return there,*
*till they have watered the earth,*
*making it fertile and fruitful*
*Giving seed to the one who sows*
*and bread to the one who eats,*
*So shall my word be*
*that goes forth from my mouth;*
*It shall not return to me void,*
*but shall do my will,*
*achieving the end for which I sent it.*
*(Is 55:6–11)*

# Introduction

*The Word became flesh and made his dwelling among us, and we saw his glory.* (Jn 1:14)

Recently a priest who works with the Chinese community in and around the Bay area experienced a tragedy within his community. A young woman, 42, secretary to his work with Catholic Chinese, died. She had undergone what should have been a routine surgery and never came out of the anesthetic. The priest waited in the hospital room for her return. In his hand he held a balloon that said "Get well soon!"

About seven hours later a nurse came and told him the sad news. The priest felt angry at the balloon. He did not know what to do with it. When he left the hospital he threw the balloon in the back seat of his car. Five days later, as he drove to the woman's funeral, the balloon was still there. On the way he reflected on the homily he was to give. A realization came over him. He was the one who needed to get well, needed healing of his pain, his anger, his sense of confusion. And if he needed healing so did the entire community gathering for the funeral. In his homily, with tears, he presented the balloon to the community. "Get well soon!"

This story offers one of myriad ways in which the incarnate God is present to us, healing, loving, inviting,

consoling, challenging us...giving us balloons. God inter-
mingles with all of our activities and we will find God
woven there, or not at all. This book is an effort to help
us reflect on our experience, enabling us to discover the
"dearest freshness deep down things."

This seems to be a critical need in our era, when religion and life seem all but totally divorced from one
another. My desire is to help make the connection. The
method of reflection into which I invite the reader flows
naturally out of my entire spiritual life, for I am deeply,
inexcusably Ignatian. For the past ten years I have
worked extensively with a wonderful group of predominantly lay Christian people in a program offering The
Spiritual Exercises in Everyday Life. Each year about
eighty people make the entire Spiritual Exercises of St.
Ignatius for nine months as they go about the affairs of
their daily lives. This experience of guiding people in
prayer, not in some remote place of retreat, but
enmeshed in what they do each day, every year, has
helped to form in them a mentality, a conviction that
God is not necessarily found somewhere else,,as in some
remote desert, but walking our streets, sharing our lives,
laughing with our joys, crying our tears.

We discover the heart of the *Spiritual Exercises of St.*
*Ignatius* in its conclusion. The fourth and final week or
stage of the Exercises ends with a prayer experience
aimed at helping us discover "God in all things." The
*Contemplatio ad Amore* presents a variety of ways to
pray over one's life and the retreat now being completed
that evoke a response of enormous, deep, continuous
gratitude. The proper response to the discovery of God
is, indeed, gratitude. Often, in directing others in retreat
I suggest that they spend the final day or so of the retreat
simply being aware, looking, tasting, touching, smelling
whatever is around them and saying "Wow!...wow to

everything, thanks for everything, the toothpaste, the sunrise, the sausages, the friends, even the challenges that constitute each one's unique life. This book invites the reader to experience living in this fourth week in growing awareness of and gratitude for this all-pervasive presence of God.

My reflections also arise, in great part, from the experiences of the parish in which I have been privileged to live and work, to worship and serve for the past nine years. The stories of St. Leo are wondrous and plentiful. I offer them, not so that you may write our parish history or, even less, my autobiography, but as a way of inviting you to touch prayerfully the mystery of *your* life, wherever you are. I invite you to do the same, perhaps with more depth than I will muster, celebrating the divine dimension of your life. I do this with the profound belief that all of us need to see life as so much more than just "one damn thing after another." I only know how to speak of God concretely, in the stories of a Word made flesh. I firmly believe that God "pitched a tent" right next to ours and we will discover that God as we discover the meanings of our own copious, fertile, transcendent stories.

Much has been written in recent years about the theology of storytelling. John Shea, among many others, has created an abundant appreciation for narrative as revelatory of the divine storyteller. Others will use myths, legends, apocryphal accounts to speak to them of meanings too deep for ordinary words. I prefer to use the stories of my own experience, inviting the reader to undertake the same exciting reflection. In such reflection we touch what Karl Rahner has called "the mysticism of daily life." My hope is for each reader to develop a personal way of telling his or her own story with a richness previously unappreciated.

This storytelling, while conversational, need not be
shallow. Our Judeo-Christian tradition speaks of Exodus,
the experience of our Hebraic ancestors being led from
slavery to freedom, from Egypt to a promised land.
Centuries later they told the stories to pass on their
experiences now shaped by the lens of faith. They told
the wonderful deeds God had done for them. In much
the same fashion, each of us lives and benefits by telling
the stories of our own exodus, our own journey from
slavery to freedom, our journey with our God from a
variety of slaveries into a growing personal freedom.
When we fail to appreciate our personal exodus story,
when we are unable to acknowledge the miracle our life
has been, we remain impotent to celebrate the gift of
life and love our God shares with us.

Catherine Mowry LaCugna's recent excellent book on
the Trinity, *God For Us* (HarperCollins, 1991), reminds us
forcibly that all of our considerations of God need to be
rooted in relationship. The God we believe in and worship is a God who is *for us*, constantly relating to us,
ever intimately involved with our lives. God shows us a
face in Jesus, gives us life in the Spirit, brings us back to
God through that face, that Spirit. For the most part in
the pages that follow I do not try to distinguish between
the voice of God, the love of Jesus, and the bond of the
Spirit. I do not try to distinguish which of three divine
persons is involved in this or that specific interaction.
Rather, my hope is to deepen the reader's conviction
that God, who is essentially community, loves us too
much to leave us alone. The divine life is active in history, never simply locked up in itself, never disentangled
from human affairs. Though these reflections are rooted
in theology, I am not an academic theologian. I believe in
the need for a pastoral voice helping us be attentive to
the profound mystery of God *for us*. I urge the reader to

share Catherine LaCugna's primary concern that God not be considered a long time ago, a long way away, but right here, right now, *for us*!

Let me return to the story with which I began this introduction. We all hold balloons in our hands. God has given them to us, often through our interaction with one another. We need to see and celebrate the balloons, even those that come cloaked in the mystery of suffering or death. We can pass these balloons on to others as all of us struggle to "get well soon." Put less poetically, it is only by reflecting on, naming, celebrating the ways we experience God that we have anything significant to say to another about that God. The Word dwells with us. Come, see and hear that word with me.

Let me end with a word of prayer for this book and for its readers.

For all who give you a face,
Oh God,
by spreading your love in the world,
we thank you.

For all who give you hands,
Oh God,
by doing their best toward their sisters and brothers,
we thank you.

For all who give you a mouth,
Oh God,
by defending the weak and the oppressed,
we thank you.

For all who give you eyes,
Oh God,
by seeing every bit of love,

in the heart of woman and man,
we thank you.

For all who give you a heart,
Oh God,
by preferring the poor to the rich,
the weak to the strong,
we thank you,

For all who give to your poverty,
Oh God,
the look of hope for the Kingdom,
we thank you.

For all who reveal you,
simply by what they are,
Oh God,
because they reflect your beauty in their lives,
we thank you.

# 1.

## The Religious Dimension of Everyday Experience: The Laborious Search

*Thus let us enter together on the path of charity in search of (God) of whom it is said: "Seek God's face evermore," for this is the sacred safe compact into which I, in the presence of the Lord our God shall enter with those who read what I am writing, in all my writings, especially in the present one where we are investigating the unity of the Trinity....For nowhere else is the error more dangerous, the* search more laborious, *and the results more rewarding* (St. Augustine, *De trinitate*, 15:28. 51).

To begin our laborious search for the Trinity ( the presence of God, the experience of Christ, the power of God's Spirit) in the ordinary experiences of our everyday lives, I first invite you into an experience of prayer. Please take the time to enter.

Sit comfortably in a chair. Imagine yourself seated in front of a small television screen. You are alone in the room. The screen is blank. When you turn the set on you see yourself seated as you are. It is as if you are outside yourself, looking at yourself seated before the screen. When the picture begins, it moves backwards over the past twenty-four hours of your life. You watch slowly, without judging, just seeing the moments of your day starting from the present moment, up to a full day ago. Remember carefully, in as much detail as you can, what it was like, ...the people you saw, the meals you ate, the activities you were engaged in. Recall even the hours of sleep, ...the peace, or lack of it, your dreams, your mood upon awakening. Take some time to slowly go over these hours...again, not judging, just noticing, savoring, relishing, reliving.

God is intimately involved in this day. The word is enfleshed here, or not at all.

Take a few moments now to pick out just one part of that day...one conversation, one meal, one experience... something significant, or problematic...something delightful or painful. Any moment, or piece with which you want to spend a few moments. Go back and recall it as vividly and in as much detail as possible. Is there anything for which you want to thank God? Anything for which you are sorry? Anything in which you want/need to ask for advice or help? Take some time to do that now.

Is there anything God wants to say to you? Take a moment, be still, and listen.

Spend about five more minutes just being with that part of your day, praying in whatever way you are moved to.

This exercise may be the most fruitful thing about this chapter, or even the entire book, but let me move on to what will basically be a reflection on this mode of prayer.

I have never done this exercise myself nor led a group of people in it without discovering that there is much more in any one twenty-four-hour period of our lives than we are inclined to realize. There is often a richness, a challenge, a joy, not noticed the first time through it. There are some precious moments in every day. One of the first times I ever did this exercise I recalled a young woman, a student in an English literature class, who had raised her hand in class that day. A painfully shy person, she had never offered to respond before. Here, in April, eight months into the school year she did, and at the time I had missed it, had not noticed. Only in this moment of quiet review did I realize how important it would have been for me to acknowledge the bravery of her raised hand, and invite her to do so again. Something truly significant had happened unnoticed as I rushed through yet another endless round of things to be done, tasks to be performed, appointments to keep. We all slide into the same haste traps. But life is rich and needs to be savored: once savored, the fruits are sweet indeed. Sometimes the experience may be painful, but without such reflection the pain goes underground, unappreciated, undealt with, unfruitful.

In many ways the most profound theological work of the past decade or so is Alice Walker's *The Color Purple*. Everyone who reads the book underlines the same passage in which two women are talking about God. Shug reminds us that the only God we are likely to find in church will be the one we brought in with us. People really do not come to church to find God, but rather to share what has been found before they came. As she tells us so powerfully, God gets really (angry) if we can walk by the color purple and not notice. Unless we can find the face of God, of Jesus woven into our experience, we do not have very much to share or celebrate when we come together in a church. We need to notice the Christ that "plays in ten thousand places, lovely in limbs and lovely in eyes not his."

People as diverse as Thomas Berry and Robert

Fulghum articulate the need to look more carefully at our experience. Berry focuses on our cosmic experience and the need for us to see the world not just as a series of events but as a "story." Human life, collectively and, by extension, individually goes somewhere, unfolds, is a process *with meaning*. I want to help us look for that meaning. Robert Fulghum, the armchair philosopher of kindergarten wisdom, suggests eloquently that we need to look, not so much for the meaning *of life*, as for the meaning *in life*. Both Berry and Fulghum acknowledge a profound need to pay attention to our lives as we pass through them.

In fact our entire religious tradition depends upon doing so. Our story begins with Moses noticing a bush is burning and not being consumed. When he notices, the bush speaks to him. This is not really rare; bushes speak all the time but we fail to listen. ( I have a friend who knows that when she dies and sees God, God will look like a Hoover vacuum cleaner. She always talks to her vacuum cleaner when she needs a space for prayer. Her vacuum cleaner often talks back. Recently she moved to a much smaller house with few carpets but she vacuums as much as ever.) But to get back to burning bushes and the Moses story. Imagine Moses talking to the bush and the bush says to him:

"Take off your shoes, Moses, you are standing on Holy Ground."

And Moses replies (it's not in the book but he must have said it):
"But this is the ground I always stand on!"
And the bush replies: "Right!"
We all stand on holy ground all the time. Moses talks to God out in the fields where he watches his flocks, not

in the temple. Go on with the story: I imagine Moses coming home that night and saying to his wife:

"Honey, we're going back to Egypt! We're going to set our people free."

And she says,"We can't go back there; you're wanted for murder."

Moses says,"I know but we have to go."

"Who told you?"

"A bush!"

"Right."

It is not easy to trust our experiences and build our lives on them. Something profound about our entire religious story lies buried beneath that simple narrative. How many bushes over how many centuries might have spoken to others before one man, Moses, had the courage to listen, and respond? I love the rabbinical legend that suggests that Abraham was the twelfth person asked, the first to respond. Before Mary said her, "Be it done," were there young maidens who had conversations with angels only to discount them as a bad dream or something that they ate? Abraham, Moses and Mary are not all that different from you or me.

Christian life is not a matter of creating God, but of experiencing the God who is present all the time and then of having the courage to trust what we experienced and to build our life on it. It is so easy to say, "That must have been my imagination," or "It was only the fervor of a retreat," or "No one would believe it anyway." I would love to have a dollar for every person who has come to my office and said something like, "You are not going to believe this, but once when I was young. . ." or "You will probably think I'm crazy, but. . ." or "I've never told anyone this before, but . . ." and then go on to tell me a profound, deep, disturbing, challenging, but in some ways very ordinary story of God's involvement in his or her life. God acts often, but we can be too busy to notice. The religious challenge is to notice our experience, to trust it, to build our lives on it.

This need is also mine. Once when I was preaching on the feast of the Holy Trinity, about to explain the mystery for the first time in history, I waxed eloquent about the presence of God in our midst. I used the titles *Life Giver, Pain Bearer, and Love Maker*—my words for the Triune God who is not so far away, with examples of each. I utilized many of the stories I will use in this chapter about the God we know in relationship to us (whatever we may not know about how God is all by Godself). After the homily that day we were planning to celebrate a fiftieth anniversary for a wonderful Filipino couple, Sal and Bing. Though marginally aware of their presence I did not fully notice the couple and their entourage until I finished talking. When I called them forward before the community I audibly gasped. Bing was garbed in a bright gold dress; her husband Sal wore an ethnic white dress shirt. They were accompanied by many relatives and friends— in fact, flower girls, ring bearer, their original best man and maid of honor who had flown from the Philippines for the occasion, all of this from a very poor family.

When we first met this lovely couple at St. Leo parish two or three years earlier, they had come to the parish for assistance, asking perhaps for a small job they could do for some financial help. They were displaced, unsettled, dirt poor and they told a story of a life of almost incredible hardship, especially their escape from their homeland immediately after their marriage during the war. Still very poor, they were living in subsidized housing across the street from the church. But here they were beaming with joy, dressed in splendor, coming up the aisle of the church, their hands joined, surrounded by people who loved them. All my words about the God in our midst seemed instantly superfluous. As they exchanged their wedding vows, we had before us a sign of the enduring, faithful, "good times and bad, sickness and health, until death" presence of God in our midst. We use such language all the time to describe a married couple's sacramental relationship to each other and to us, and now, suddenly, our theology seemed more than true. My words were not needed; all we had to do was see what was right there before us, and celebrate it. I stood, silent, dumbstruck, for a lengthy interval before I could go on, with tears streaming down my cheeks. If we do not notice such things and weep, God cannot get at us at all.

Again, the invitation, indeed the joy, is to see, celebrate and trust the One who is in our midst. Morton Kelsey, an Episcopal priest and Jungian analyst, who taught for years at Notre Dame, has detailed about fifteen different ways in which we experience the **Transcendent.** I have held on to some of his categories and added my own. Gerald May, somewhere, calls such human events **Unitive Experiences**–moments when we are one, together with our selves, with God, with the universe. I am inclined to speak more simply of experiences of God.

## VARIETIES OF EXPERIENCE

*Dreams:* Anyone who has read Morton Kelsey would expect that his first category, and so mine, is Dreams. I am convinced, along with so many Jungians, that God visits us when we sleep, as he did both Joseph's in either testament. In a dream God invited Paul to take his incipient faith to Macedonia. I do not easily or often catch my dreams and I have never been able to do the kind of steady reflection on them that I admire in others, but sometimes even I notice.

Once at the end of a retreat I had a marvelous, epic-novel dream. I was playing basketball (a frequent metaphor for my life since, when younger, I fancied myself a player). In the dream, although the gym was very dark, I was extremely "hot," while warming up. I threw in shots from every corner, under my legs, behind my back...everything swished. As game time approached I realized that my team had two men, and four women. Our opponents had four men and two women. It dawned on me that each team had to play with two men and one woman at a time. That meant that I would have to play the entire game, and I was forty-six years old! All the elation of my imminent stardom while warming up evaporated. I was literally "undermanned." The dream was a fitting conclusion to a retreat in which I had wrestled with my struggles in a previous parish. In almost classical Jungian categories it clearly suggested that I, who had always been able to enjoy my feminine side, thrived on reading poetry and on acting with compassion, was weak in the stereotypical masculine virtues, like strength, courage, and the ability to take a stand even if someone was offended. The dream presented, quite truly, a message from God.

Not long ago I celebrated a funeral for the husband of an African American woman in our parish. Some weeks later I visited her and she told me a marvelous story. The day before my visit she had attended a funeral of a lifetime friend. The night before the funeral she had a dream in which her husband was down in the basement, whistling, singing, and happy as he had never been during the final years of his life. She went to the basement and found him building a lovely pine box, getting the corners just so and sanding down the edges. She awoke full of peace, knowing that her husband, wherever he was now, was truly happy. At the funeral she was astounded to discover that her friend was being buried in a beautiful pine box, exactly like the one her husband worked on in her dream. And the friend was being laid in a grave immediately adjacent to her husband's. Consoled by the dream, my friend was overjoyed after this funeral. Through dream and reality God had assured her of her husband's peace.

Many times in spiritual direction or in less formal conversations I have heard similar dreams. Some were less startling, but each contained a word that needed to be heard, an insight longed for, a challenge necessary. Even for those of us who do not easily recall our dreams, God sometimes breaks through and is present to us.

*Human Love:* The second category of human experience in which we discover God is Love, human love. I believe what the Letter of John asserts, that "God is love, and whoever remains in love remains in God and God in him (or her)" (1 Jn 4:16). Often we fail to reflect on this. I suppose this is true of any kind of real love, but I discover it especially true in experiences of being loved when we do not deserve it, have not earned it, when we even have broken some trust that would make love's absence understandable. It is difficult to tell stories because our experiences of love are so personal. However, Jesus is the incarnation of love, the love of God spoken in our midst, so every experience of human love is an experience of God.

I pride myself on being collaborative in ministry. I try my best to include the staff I work with in every decision affecting their ministry or lives. Often I am completely uninvolved in matters that are properly theirs. And, in honesty, the people I work with have appreciated this. But a year or so ago, I made a mistake, unconsciously, of responding over the phone to something that touched into another's ministry. I made a snap decision without even thinking to tell her, much less ask her. Two days later she came into my office. She was in tears and trembling because confrontation was not her favorite mode of communication. She sat with me and told me how much she respected me, appreciated my work and my support, but that I had hurt her deeply and made a serious mistake. But because of what she thought of me, the mistake, finally, did not matter. She trusted me enough to tell me that. She hoped that I would change the decision, but whether I did or not, she forgave me. It was easy to change the decision. What was more difficult was accepting and appreciating the courage and the love she showed in speaking to me that way. And in that love was God, who forgives but challenges, corrects but affirms.

I have believed for years that the sacrament of reconciliation is most frequently conferred within the sacrament of marriage, because I cannot imagine any love relationship working for long unless each party is able to forgive the other, whether they deserve, earn, or even appreciate the forgiveness. The gift of forgiving love that couples or any friends give to each other signifies and incarnates the gift of God's love to us.

For the first time in my life I recently began to live alone. It was not by choice but due to the vagaries of the contemporary church. Shortly after I moved in I was sitting watching TV alone on a Saturday night when a knock at the door got me up and out of feeling sorry for myself. I went to the door to discover the entire staff of people I work with and their spouses, along with several other friends—a crowd of about fifty people charging into my home for a spontaneous housewarming. They brought all the food and drink, a wonderful present for my home, and a deep abiding sense of being loved. For them it was a party; for me (and probably for most of them too) it was a religious experience. God was undeniably present.

If you want to be aware of God in the very fabric of life, recall the times you have been loved when you so easily could not have been.

*Childlike Simplicity:* God is also discovered in childlike simplicity. An entire book, *Mr. God, This is Anna,* presents God, revealed in insights of children. My favorite experience of this occurred some years ago as I walked around the neighborhood of the parish where I was working. I stopped to talk to a young mother, whose five-year old daughter was trying out her new jump rope. Recalling my younger days I began to help the child by demonstrating simple technique. When I gave her back the rope, she jumped, made it, and her mother and I clapped wildly. She continued to jump, over and over, each success accompanied with our clapping until she was able to do five or six jumps in a row. She went off to jump alone while we visited. About three minutes later the little girl came back, dragging her rope, looking forlorn, her head hanging. She said one of the most profound things I ever heard: "Mom, I can do it, but I need lots of clapping." Her words reflect a deep existential truth about human existence: We can do it, but someone needs to clap. I cannot now recall what was happening in my life at the time, but her words cut to my heart. I knew that I could do what I was doing, but I desperately needed more clapping. This girl's childlike simplicity revealed God to me.

A friend with whom I work tells of driving home one day and waiting at a four-way stop sign. She watched as a woman got off a bus, looking absolutely exhausted. Kitty-corner from her stood a young girl, dressed in grownup clothes, with a huge purse, shoes many sizes too large, a dress and hat, also voluminous, excited to meet her mother coming home from work. She was dressed in her mother's clothes and quite proud of her garb. Clearly the young girl had been warned not to cross or go out into the street, so she danced and waved, and yelled. But her bedraggled mother did not notice for the longest time. Cars at all four corners waited, many watching the drama unfold, until finally the weary mother looked across the street, saw her dancing daughter, and broke into, first a smile, then a run to the girl whom she swept up in her arms in a fond embrace. A simple, lovely human story. A profound experience of the God who comes to us as a little child, meets us in our various states of fatigue, calls us out of ourselves to notice a whole world dressed up to meet us on every corner.

*Art:* The transcendent God also reveals the Godself to us through the creativity of human genius. Jacques Maritain explained many years ago that art is the sharing of experience through some medium. The artist (painter, poet, sculptor, songwriter) has an experience or a variety of experiences. He or she captures that experience in an art form. Sometime, a month, a year, an eon later another person comes to the work of art, sees (or listens, touches, hears) and shares in the original experience of the artist. When two human spirits reach across time, space, culture, gender, race, and every boundary we can build to touch each other, God is deeply present.

I frequently recall my return to the seminary in 1958 after my mother died. It is all but impossible to convey the feeling of a pre-Vatican II seminary to one who has not experienced it. I arrived about 9:00 P.M., and the community was already in "Grand Silence," so no one spoke a word to me. I went to my cubicle. I tried to sleep. I arose the next morning, cleaned up, went to first visit, spent an hour "praying" in my room, then to mass, breakfast, and the cleanup that followed. All this time no one said, "Hello, I'm sorry about your mother; how are you?" Not a word. My closest friends nodded, or snuck a smile, but no truly human interaction occurred. The most devastating experience of my life had happened, and no one near me paid any attention. It felt like, as Robert Frost says, "Since they were not the one dead they went on about their business."

Eventually, at 9:00 A.M., fully twelve hours after my arrival back "home," I went to class. I presumed the class, from which I had been absent for two weeks, would take up where they left off the day before. Only in hindsight do I realize the teacher, acting almost humanly in that inhuman environment, had very carefully planned the class for me. We were studying Emily Dickinson. The first words I heard, then, were from a poem of hers:

> The bustle in a house
> The morning after death,
> Is solemnest of industries,
> Enacted upon earth.
>
> The sweeping up the heart,
> And putting love away,
> We shall not want to use again,
> Until eternity.

I thank God that someone in Massachusetts one hundred years ago, knew what I was experiencing in Oregon many years later. I was overwhelmed by words that reached across a century, so grateful that this reclusive woman in Amherst knew what I was feeling even if no one else seemed to know or care. Someone knew and gave a damn. Her spirit touched mine, and I was, for the moment, all right, for I was not alone.

Through the years many other poems have touched me in much the same way, the right word at the right time from someone who knew what I knew and was able to say it in a fashion that united me both with the poet and with God.

In a quite different way I recall the profound experience of seeing Michaelangelo's *David*, in Florence. Those who have seen it will remember walking toward that statue through a series of unfinished statues, pieces of an arm, or a torso, a full head with an unfinished body—a series of parts of the human person emerging from stone. With unspeakable wonder, then, the magnificent, fully formed, perfectly shaped, gigantic figure of David stands in the midst of these lesser, unfinished pieces. He looks alive, every sinew real, vibrant, unimaginably perfect. Words fail me here, as they did when I stood there, but never anywhere else have I been so profoundly moved by the wonder of the human body and the artist's uncanny ability to capture, beyond words, the work of God's hand. I am told that when Michaelangelo carved the *David*, he left the very tip of the head unfinished so it would be clear this was, indeed, a human work and not the work of God. I have always hoped that story is true, but did not check to see!

Different people have different tastes, different cultural expectations, different interests in art. I invite you, whatever form of art most touches your spirit, to pause a moment here to recall a time when a song, a symphony, a drama, a novel, a painting helped you touch the divine.

*The Experience of Community:* God's Spirit binds us together in every profound experience of community, unites us into even the most unlikely bonds of love. Whenever the power in a group reaches beyond the sheer results produced by the people there, and speaks, instead, of some Spirit beyond them, God is there.

Our parish staff some years ago had, as staffs do, a very painful episode. For a variety of reasons we were unable to relate well to each other. Two people had experienced a major argument which reached beyond the specific moment of anger. People sided with one or the other staff member. Others simply distanced themselves from the entire painful reality. We became dysfunctional, or perhaps the dysfunction that had been there for some time was no longer deniable. We realized the need to set aside some time, hire a facilitator and work through the pain of the present if any future was to be ours. We did so and on a verbal level explored what happened, what led to the argument and what we might do to prevent similar occurrences in the days ahead. At the end of the day we enacted a kind of psychodrama. Each of us stood in the room in relative proximity to every other person in a way that captured how we were experiencing our relationship with the group before the blow-up. People took different stances: one person was halfway out the door, one stood on a chair, apart and above, looking at the others with curiosity, one was on the ground feeling beaten down by the experience. I dramatized myself as rushing frantically from one to another, with no real plan or order but trying to fix everything and make it all right, not siding with anyone or anything (a perfect Sufi Two, for those interested in such things).

When we finished dramatizing the past, we were invited by our facilitator to rearrange into whatever positions demonstrated how we would like to be related in the future. We regrouped for a few moments. Eventually we were in one large, embracing glob, each trying to touch every other one, with the arms of those most estranged most tightly bound now. As we gathered in this way, each person began to cry. I can still feel the tears running down my face, hearing the sobs of others as we enacted who we would like, at our best, to be. The Spirit of God bound us together in love. Though it would take much work to become, in fact the community we were for that moment in hope, it was profoundly clear that our God had given us an enormously helpful nudge in the right direction.

*Religious Ritual:* Some of our finest experiences of community do occur in church, especially at funerals, or weddings, or moments of special celebration where the gathered community is focused by some shared reason to be together. This realization eases me into another category of religious experience, *religious ritual behavior.* Despite Alice Walker's assertion, we do sometimes meet God in church or within the rituals of the church. I held this topic until now because there are so many other places where the interaction happens that to start with "churchy things" would be to feed into our false presumptions. But sometimes, sadly not often enough, we do truly discover God in that community gathered for worship. For most Roman Catholics, every once in a while, in the midst of the thousand times we have said or heard the words, the priest holds up the consecrated bread and says:"This is the Lamb of God, the One who takes away our Sins," and we are overwhelmed by the reality. Sometimes we are struck with the amazing truth of what we have begun to take for granted because we have done it so frequently. Sometimes we listen to the scriptures read at eucharist, and what we hear speaks directly to the concern we brought with us to church. The reading becomes truly what it purports to be, *word of God,* for us.

Lately I have had the opportunity to celebrate eucharist several times and not be the presider. As I watched I was surprised to discover how relatively few people receive from the cup. I have always had a sense of Jesus saying to me, to us "Can you drink this cup?" It is important to me to say "Yes!" In the multicultural community where I serve, with many people of different races, many mentally ill, many with disease and pain, it becomes important to me to ask: "Can I drink the cup they just drank?" Sometimes I am overwhelmed by the profundity of sharing in that cup. Jesus invites me to let his blood flow in my veins, his life continue to be lived through me. Most frequently I take this miracle for granted, but from time to time the awesome presence of Christ in this familiar gesture really works and does communicate God's love for me.

One of the parish council members at St. Leo often tells me how he sits on the side aisle every Sunday because it gives him the best view of people from two sides coming forward and returning from communion, for within this moment he most discovers God. He dwells on the faces, the diversity of young, old, brown, red, white, black, straight, gay, rich, poor, sick or stable, each reacting in unique wonder to the mystery just received. The experience sustains him throughout the week.

I will mention other specific examples later in the book. For me the ritual behavior where God is most often felt occurs at funerals. One December eighth, we had to substitute a funeral for the feast of the Immaculate Conception mass. A young man had been hit by a bus, and killed instantly. He was a very important

part of our community, a mildly retarded, amazingly cre-
ative member of our parish. John had an uncanny ability
to make up stories, telling different ones to different
people, somehow remembering which people heard
which story. His fantasy life was incredibly rich. He was
a radio announcer for the local soccer team, and an assis-
tant manager for the baseball team. He taught special
education (at the school which he, in fact, attended). He
was also a disk jockey and a campaign manager for a
political candidate. Each career gave rise to a different
story for a different audience. At his funeral we took
time to tell some of these stories, to sing and celebrate
John's life. His parents and sister heard wonderful things
about their son and brother they had not heard before.
Much consolation came to them from a community that
obviously appreciated John's uniqueness as much as his
family had. By coincidence a thirty-five year old man
came to church that night to celebrate Mary's feast after
an absence from the church for several years.
Overwhelmed by the experience of a celebratory death,
an enormous outpouring of love for an obviously fragile
young man, with songs and tears and laughter, this surprised young man experienced God bringing him to his
knees in humble faith.

When the funeral was over the visitor came with tears
in his own eyes and told me how touched he had been. I
suggested he tell the deceased boy's mother, which he
did. This religious ritual, these funeral rites consoled a
family, invited a deep new-found faith in a wandering
soul, and enlivened the lives of many. More than two or
three were present and God was in our midst.

Religious ritual behavior also occurs outside of church
buildings. This was brought home to me in a wondrous
fashion through an experience three years ago. One
morning a parishioner and friend confided that his

daughter had taken an overdose of sleeping pills. She was at the hospital in a coma. Throughout the day the coma continued. Early that evening he called and asked me if I would come and baptize his daughter. Her mother deeply wanted it. My reaction was quite orthodox. I reasoned to myself that if the girl had wanted to be baptized she would have asked when she was well. She had some excellent theological education, some good experience of church, but had never on her own come forward to request baptism. What business did I have to force it on her when she was unconscious? But that was a poor time to use theological reasoning with the parents, so on my way to another engagement I went to the hospital. I explained my conviction that the sacraments were not magic, but that I would certainly pray with them for their daughter's recovery and baptize her in case that was what she wanted.

The doctor was becoming concerned whether the girl would in fact pull out and recover after twelve hours of coma. So we prayed together. I took water from the emergency room sink, and poured it lightly on the young girl's head, saying the ancient, ritualistic words, "I baptize you in the name of the Father, and of the Son, and of the Holy Spirit." To our amazement the girl instantaneously opened her eyes, and said, "Amen." She began to sit up, smiling, and said, "Thank You!" All my rationalistic theology melted away in the power of that moment. The miracle of the moment was not isolated, for when she was fully recovered the young woman continued to come to church and to celebrate the sacraments. Eventually she married a Catholic young man, and I had the deep joy of baptizing their first child three years later. We do sometimes meet God in religious ritual behavior.

The results need not be so dramatic. Sometimes the

faith involved simply in celebrating the rite allows for God's powerful presence. One very active member of our parish had been depressed for almost a year. His wife was worried, tired and needed support; his young daughter was confused. The wife asked if she could invite some of their parish friends to come and pray with her husband one Sunday evening. She urged me to join them. I heartily agreed. That Sunday about sixty people came to sit with, hope for, pray alongside of this couple. We are not a "charismatic" parish in the usual sense. That evening our prayer was quiet and deep. Love permeated the room. We did not know what else to do for our friend, but we could be with him. We could love him. We could hold him before God in our hearts. No dramatic cure took place. Slowly over the next months most of the depression subsided, although he still lives with it and probably always will. This moment of celebrating the Rite of Anointing allowed us to experience God caring about him and his family when we did not know what else to do.

Obviously we cannot ever exhaust the places where God may be found. Let me mention here two others, one of which will be expanded into a chapter by itself. Out of my experiences at St. Leo I am convinced that we find God whenever we hear *the call to justice* and whenever we make honest *contact with the poor.*

*The Call to Justice:* Experiences of God are not always light or funny. Regularly I am urged out of various complacencies to care about the hurts of people around me. I am by nature a pleaser, a healer, a builder. I had to learn to be a rabble-rouser, when rousing was called for. Each time that I have the courage to speak or act out the gospel invitation to justice, I know God's touch. When I heard one morning on National Public Radio (from the voice of a California Jesuit who had spent time at St. Leo) about the tragic deaths of six El Salvadoran Jesuits and two of their companions, God touched me in my deepest truest self. I had for years been semi-active in various protests about our government's complicity in that tragic civil war and had been touched before by all-too-many deaths—Rutillo Grande, Archbishop Romero, four American women. None of these had really urged me to fruitful action on behalf of justice. After the Jesuits' deaths I found myself much more outspoken about the atrocities for which we, Americans, were largely responsible. I even uncharacteristically organized and spoke at a rally downtown in front of our congressman's office. I felt a power of God calling me out of myself. Such things have happened in lesser ways before and since, and I suspect they happen to others who are as reluctant as I to take a prophet's role. Before we go on you may want to test your own experience of this particularly discomforting presence of God. Have you ever experienced God inviting you to speak or act in ways that call for change? Have you risked misunderstanding, or unpopularity and known God was involved in the risk?

*The Poor:* We will take more time later to consider our experience of finding God's face in the poor, but here let me share a single experience. Not long ago a woman from one of the shelters near the parish came to see me. Usually the woman at our desk can take care of financial need or crisis far better than I, but this woman wanted to see "the priest." It took a while to discover what exactly her specific need was. She began by asking if we could get her a house. Now, we do many things but we cannot easily buy houses for people, though through

*Habitat for Humanity* we sometimes can help build them. But she wanted help today.

After a few moments of conversation it became more clear that what she really wanted was money to do her laundry. That was easy enough to take care of. I have been haunted ever since by the next segment of our conversation. What made her think about housing was her experience that morning of wandering around our Hilltop neighborhood and seeing all the unused, boarded up houses, more than three hundred in our immediate vicinity. She asked me, "*Why can't we use them in the meantime?*" That, "*in the meantime*," has become the word of God for me, spoken with an insight beyond her awareness but not her sensitivity. What exactly is the "meantime"? The time between now and the parousia? The time between now and some kinder and gentler nation? Or is it simply this time now as we continue to be mean to one another. This woman's question has for me been a question from God that I would not have heard with the same force if it had not come from "the poor."

I could go on and on. At this point I want only to suggest the presence of God consoling, disturbing, imagining, and ever-present, giving life, sharing wounds, building love all around and deep within us. God is enfleshed in us and in our world. God pitches a tent next to ours. Certainly my words and stories are of no use to whoever reads this book unless each reader begins to recall his or her own stories. What I write will do no good at all unless each person begins to notice, trust, and build a deeper, fuller life on such experiences. God is present all around us, and our task is to notice the experiences, to trust them, and to build our future on them.

# 2.

## Will Anybody Lift Me Up?
## Finding God in Personal
## and Liturgical Prayer

*Brothers and sisters, through the blood of Jesus we have the right to enter the sanctuary, by a new way which he has opened for us, a living opening through the curtain, that is to say, his body* (Heb 10:19).

The letter to the Hebrews suggests that we no longer have only a temple, a holy of holies, where a priest goes once a year to touch God, but that now the way is opened for all of us to find God, to find the holy everywhere. The holy of holies is the world in which we live, every part and parcel of it. We cannot decide ahead of time that God is here or there, but need to be open to the Christ we will find in his body, his people, or the world, which has been called by Sally McFague, "God's body." We cannot exclude or too quickly dismiss places of worship. Prayer might be described as expanding ever more widely our horizons of worship, awe, wonder and gratitude.

A woman going through our catechumenate a few years ago shared a marvelous personal faith-story with us. She was a bus driver in downtown Tacoma, usually at night. Her route and time all but guaranteed a frightening undertaking. Over the time of her catechumenal

experience, she developed a prayerful technique, decid-
ing that everyone who boarded her bus each night was
Jesus in disguise. The more frightening the person was,
the more clever the disguise. When she was tempted to
be disturbed by a mean, dispirited, drunk or drugged
passenger, she prayed beneath her breath, "Boy, Jesus,
that's really a good one; nobody would recognize you,"
or "That's your best disguise yet." Her fears were
reduced and, more importantly, she found herself able to
treat each passenger with a respect some of them
received nowhere else in their lives. She found a living
opening through the curtain by which God's face was
revealed to her. This practice begins to reveal whatever I
would have to say about prayer.

In this chapter, I will reflect on prayer, expanding
what I began in the previous chapter. I will develop
more carefully one of the ways in which we may find
God in personal or communal, religious ritual behavior. I
will speak about finding the presence of God, the face of
Christ, the life of their Spirit within my own heart and in
my unique relationship with that God.

If a thousand people write about prayer, all will do so
differently because we all pray differently, and God
prays in us differently. These can only be my reflections,
true for me, and perhaps helpful to you. But I would
assert that, down deep, whatever else anyone says about
prayer, at least from a Christian perspective, it must have
something to do with finding in the story of Jesus something of continuity with my story. The story of Jesus that
we tell over and over again, meshes with my personal
understanding of myself in my very real world with all its
relationships, joys and struggles.

As in the previous chapter, I begin with prayer. I invite
you to read slowly the following scriptural text:

Then (Jesus) made the disciples get into the boat
and precede him to the other side, while he dis-
missed the crowds. After doing so, he went up on
the mountain by himself to pray. When it was
evening he was there alone. Meanwhile the boat,
already a few miles offshore, was being tossed
about by waves, for the wind was against it. During
the fourth watch of the night, he came toward
them, walking on the sea. When the disciples saw
him walking on the sea they were terrified. "It is a
ghost," they said, and they cried out in fear. At
once, Jesus spoke to them, "Take courage, it is I; do
not be afraid." Peter said to him, in reply, "Lord, if it
is you, command me to come to you on the water."
He said, "Come." Peter got out of the boat and
began to walk on the water toward Jesus. But when
he saw how strong the wind was he became frightened; and, beginning to sink, he cried out, "Lord
save me!" Immediately Jesus stretched out his hand
and caught him, and said to him, "O you of little
faith, why did you doubt?" After they got into the
boat the wind died down. Those who were in the
boat did him homage, saying, "Truly, you are the
Son of God" (Mt 14:22–33).

Enter into this passage, much as you did in the previous chapter when you reflected on the past twenty-four
hours of your day. Become quiet and, after you recall the
passage, try to gently close your eyes. Do not so much
think about the passage as enter into it. Feel yourself at
sea, in a storm.

See Jesus coming to you across the wildly waving
waters.

Imagine yourself drawn toward him, asking him to

invite you to step out into the deep, step out on the unfamiliar waves and go to him.

Hear Jesus say to you, "Come."

Then imagine yourself taking that first step, out of the boat.

Experience yourself walking on top of the sea, toward Jesus...and then your faith falters; you realize the incredible absurdity of what you are doing, and begin to sink.

Let Jesus take you gently by the hand and return you to the boat, and finally, safely to shore.

Stay with this passage for a few moments, savoring whatever strikes you in the story, wrestling with whatever questions or concerns it raises, delighting in the feeling of safety it may give you.


### THE WORD OF GOD, FOR ME

I am convinced that the significant religious question is not, "Did Jesus really walk on water two thousand years ago, and Peter with him," but, "If I am sinking will anybody lift me up?" "If I am drowning, does anyone care?" "Does God?" We need to read and study scripture. We also need to be careful about how we exegete a particular passage. We need to avoid the fundamentalist's simplistic approach to the word of God. Still, what finally matters is whether or not it is the word of God *for me*. Prayer becomes the art of discovering how these ancient stories are true, today, in my life, in the world, and the lives of those around me.

The passage we just prayed over is clearly a kind of universal parable more than a factual event in Matthew's Gospel. The early community undoubtedly had some basis of fact on which to model the story, but it is told about every disciple, for whom Peter so often stands.

Like Peter, though perhaps more gradually, we can see the story unfolding in the specifics of our lives.

All of us, at one time or another, have been out in a storm, in deep waters, tossed and turning in the waves, while Jesus seemed absent, seemed left behind, seemed busy about other tasks more important to him than we are. In the midst of our fear all of us have looked into the face of the storm, and thought we saw Jesus, thought we discerned the hand of God, thought we may have had a glimpse of one who would rescue us. Sometimes the very cloudiness of this vision left us afraid.

All of us have, in large or small ways, thought we heard the voice of Jesus inviting us, not out of the storm, but more deeply into it, inviting us to walk with him on water. We may have had the courage to take the first step, to actually try the walk, move into that love relationship, accept that job, move ourselves or our family to a new place, whatever the request might have been. Most of us, if we had the initial courage to move into the deep, new, turbulent waters, discovered very shortly that it was even more frightening than we feared; we began to sink. Again, some of us have felt the hand of God, of Jesus, taking us to safety in the boat, and eventually to shore.

I discover myself in my own circle of friends and coworkers constantly interpreting people's lives in terms of this incredible gospel story. I see a man risk everything—job, education, familiar environment,—transplanting himself from east to west coast, believing that God may be calling him to a sacramental life with a woman he scarcely knows. He has to jump out of his boat to find out the truth. I see a woman severely scarred by a painful early marriage, afraid to enter again into the same possibility of pain. But she goes out onto the waters of love and commitment, despite the fear, and is

led gently to shore. I know a woman in mid-life deeply
disturbed by the loss of a well paying job who finds the
courage to enter into an entirely new field of work, pastoral care of the sick, because it seems that God is inviting such a change. Over and over again I see people rav-
aged by various addictions, somehow rise from the bot-
tom of the waters of despair, break the surface of grace,
enter into a twelvestep program and risk a life of sobri-
ety, a condition they had never known before.

I cannot know the details of each reader's life, but I
suspect the very reading of this book attests to a life of
faith each reader has been leading and to which each
tries to be faithful. The story of Peter and Jesus on the
waves is the story of all of us. At different times we are
in different parts of the story; rarely does it all fit neatly
together. Still, the story is ours; our prayer, our entering
into relationship with God, primarily consists in discovering ourselves "in the story."

I live and work with a marvelous couple. They have
been married for thirty-five years. Early in their marriage
he was a financial consultant with a major national firm.
In the first years they moved often, and made much
money to support themselves and their five children.
The were believing, practicing, normally committed
Catholics. Also, they were people who read and prayed,
and went to whatever adult education classes were avail-
able. They were firmly settled in Tacoma, their children
were in school, and they were involved in a parish of
which they were becoming quite fond. He was asked to
transfer again. They prayed, risked, and decided not to
take the new position. He no longer had a job. She began
to work for a salary in what had been formerly a volunteer position in the parish. She returned to school to
become more professionally prepared. Their lives began
to totally change, their income to reduce, their roles to

reverse. In the ensuing years they were drawn to St. Leo parish from their more comfortable suburban one. He had not worked at a salaried position for several years and now began to give volunteer time to many social agencies in the inner city needing the kind of financial advice for which he had previously been handsomely paid. She took a position as director of social ministries in their new parish, St. Leo. They sold their quite gorgeous home on the lake, and moved into a drug infested but vital neighborhood in the inner city, near the parish. They are among the most faith-filled, joyful, alive people I know. Their lives together have been a succession of storms and new invitations to walk on those waters, first with faltering steps, sometimes moving back, then rising, and walking again. The woman admits that she is almost always afraid—afraid of the next step, the new invitation, the most recent storm, but she sees her entire life in relationship to this passage of the gospel, so she often sings, "Be Not Afraid," and moves on.

The trick of prayer is not to discern what happened in the story of Jesus in the past, but how the story is true in the intricate moments of my present life. The challenge is to know if it is, indeed, my story.

Almost any gospel passage affords the same kind of reflective possibilities. At various times in my life I have seen Jesus exhausted by the day's labors, too tired to go with his disciples to town. I see him flopped against a well at a time when no one was likely to come. Despite his exhaustion, he rises to speak to a woman, a Samaritan, a sinner, saying to himself, "Oh, no, here comes another one." Out of that awareness, I have had the strength to make one more call, one more visit, to stay an extra hour by that hospital bed.

I have seen the non-Catholic, non-parishioner, non-believer come to the rectory door and ask for something, and have felt that, "It is not right to give the children's food to dogs." I have known the outsider's insistence, and known unexpected faith called out from me that I had not before been willing to give.

I have been buried in tombs of my own making, feeling dead, and gone, no longer fit for the light of day. I have heard Jesus outside my tomb call out, "Unbind him, and let him go free." The stories of Jesus are my stories, your stories. My initial assertion about prayer as I have come to understand it, involves discovering that connection.

## THREE REFLECTIONS ON PRAYER

### *None of us thinks we pray enough, or well enough*

No one has ever come into my office and said, "I am one of the world's truly great prayers." We all feel inadequate, uncertain, sure that others have an understanding, a grace, an ability, some charism we do not possess. We all seem to compare ourselves to Teresa of Avila, or John of the Cross, though I suspect they felt the same as we. We need to learn to trust our prayer, knowing that God works uniquely in each of us. Prayer is not something we do but something God does in us.

Some years ago, I went with a now treasured friend, then a stranger, to Lesotho in southern Africa, to spend a year giving retreats and training local people to be retreat directors. Katherine and I are quite different. For the first several weeks of our working together I was overwhelmed with her prayer and my inadequacies. When we were not working, we stayed in a central mission of the Sisters of the Holy Names. I had a small cabin that once belonged to the Peace Corps. She stayed in the Provincial Sister's house just a hundred yards or so away.

Often in the mornings I would see her sitting outside in the sunshine, her Bible on her lap in quiet communion with God. I have about a forty-five second attention span and no ability to be quiet. Here I had time to pray, to prepare prayerfully for a ministry of prayer and I could not. I read, I walked, I wrote, but sitting still was beyond me. Because of the kind of work we were doing I began to feel more and more hypocritical. How could I lead others in prayer if I could not pray myself? Katherine was the real retreat director; all I could provide was comedy relief. I had all but decided to call off the charade and return to the States.

One day I spoke with Katherine about my feelings, telling her I needed to consider going home because I was not being honest with myself and the people with whom we were working. She was astounded. She was feeling somewhat the same way, and said she was about one day from saying the same thing to me. She told me how awestruck she had become at my prayerfulness, my ability to take almost every experience we had and turn it into something related to a gospel passage, or an experience of faith. She was humbled by my reflectivity, and ability to connect the everyday with the transcendent. She told me how empty she felt sitting outside every day waiting, desperately hoping for something to happen. Perhaps one of the orphan boys from the home next door would come to play. No thoughts, no movements, no consolations, nothing, as she sat there day after day. Like myself, she was feeling very phony, artificial. We laughed, and decided that in reality everyone is at least a little inadequate, a bit phony. So I admired her fidelity; she admired my insight. Both of us wanted the gift the other had.

I have reflected much on that experience. As a result of it I began to be able to see myself as a prayerful person, to acknowledge the way I prayed, and see it as good. It became truly significant for me to have someone affirm in me, not so much *my* gift of prayer, but how God was praying effectively in me. I knew for the first time my own way of prayer, a way that is not necessarily *the* way, but *a* way. Also I began to realize how terribly important it is for each person to recognize the unique way God prays in each of us.

The trick for most of us is not to discover new ways or methods of prayer, but to discover how God is already doing it in us. I do not know how to tell this to another, but I devoutly believe it helps to get the question right.

*Our task is discover how we are praying, or how God prays in us*

I have mentioned a friend who talks to her Hoover vacuum cleaner. She discovered that this machine also talks quietly to her while she vacuums. She endures as a symbol of the discovery of God's individual style as we discover our own prayer. Once I was privileged to direct a year-long retreat for an insurance broker. He could not find time in his day for prayer despite his deep desire to make *The Spiritual Exercises in Everyday Life*. He could not imagine adding an extra hour to his day, and did not want to give up jogging, which had become important to him. I asked what he did while he jogged. He talked about that being the time in which he put the day together, looked ahead at the challenges coming up, remembered the successes and foibles of the day just past, thought about his wife and daughters, and how much he loved them. He was already spending well over an hour a day in prayer, but he did not call it prayer. It was easy to gear the retreat prayer to what was already present daily in his life. God jogged with him; that was his time of prayer.

My brother, who would deny being the least bit prayerful, told me years ago that he never took the freeway driving home from work. He had small children then and knew he needed a break between office and re-entry into the hectic family life. Taking back streets gave him some added time to slow down, to switch from one part of his life to another, gave him time, in my words, to pray. I know people who take fifteen-minute showers not to get more clean but to have some time and space to themselves. A good friend plays the piano for an hour every day. The pieces are familiar and do not require specific attention. As she plays she can bring the pieces of her life into a peace. I have watched a coworker with a small baby sit for a long time gazing with incredible tenderness into the face of her nursing child. With tears in her eyes, she disappeared from her surroundings, wrapped in ecstatic prayer.

God is always praying in us, the Spirit teaching us when we do not know how, and our task is to discover how God works into the flow of our very real, very concrete lives. Where are the quiet places, the still moments where God is already getting at *us*? Where do we find ourselves challenged or consoled?

## *We are all called to holiness*

Perhaps the most helpful insight of Vatican II was that universal call to holiness, the realization that there are not classes of people in the Christian community—some who are called to be saints and others of us who are not; some are not called to union with God while others just plod along. Some are not given mystical graces, while others stay on the outside, on the edge. We are all called

to our own unique, personal, unrepeatable brand of mysticism, our unique union with God in prayer. Our task is
not making this happen but rather noticing and naming
it when it does. We each need to see and relish the quiet
spaces in our lives, the breaks from our "one damn thing
after another," existence, the ways God works with us.
Each of us faces the delightful task of acknowledging the
God who is enfleshed in, with and for us. Perhaps some
descriptive indication of what I mean by prayer, the
quest for mysticism, will help.

## DESCRIPTIVE DEFINITIONS OF PRAYER

### *Prayer Is Letting God Love Us*

When we ask ourselves why we pray we may get a
variety of answers. Sometimes we speak as though we
pray to get God to "shape up." We ask God repeatedly to
take care of something that God apparently does not
want to deal with, on the outside chance that if we ask
often and loudly enough God's mind will change. "Oh,
God," we pray, "bring peace to our world," or "help my
uncle Jack," or "end world hunger," or "let me stop
drinking." All of those are good things to pray for, but,
unreflectively, we may be asking God to do something
so that we don't have to. Our prayers of petition at
eucharist often sound like we are cajoling God rather
than committing ourselves. I believe that underneath all
of our prayers must be the hope that we, rather than
God, will be transformed so that, with God, we can do
our part to bring whatever we pray for to be.

Rather than an unarguable, theological answer to the
question, "Why do we pray?" I give only my answer. I
pray because I need to let God love me. Prayer, for me, is
essentially that. I pray because I am so inclined to forget

that I am God's beloved son. I forget that I am not alone
in the struggles of my life. I forget that the waters will
overwhelm me unless I keep my eyes on the one who is
calling me to himself across the waves. I pray because I
need regularly to remember God's love. I read scripture
to help me remember. I celebrate eucharist because it
reminds me of God's love for me, for us, in Jesus, though
I am part of a stumbling, unfaithful people. Over and
over, I come together with a community so that God can
love us to life, create clean hearts in us, make us into the
body that we say we are. I pray individually and with
communities so that I can see the face of Christ shining
in me, on me and around me.

Thus, more precisely, we may be praying, "Oh God,
help us to become more sensitive to the plight of the
poor, more aware of how blessed we are in each meal
that we share, so that, one day, we will work with you to
overcome the hunger that still plagues our world." As the
fruit of our prayer for Uncle Jack, we may also find ourselves being moved to visit Jack, spending some time as
a healing presence in his hospital room. Perhaps through
us, God can care for and even heal him.

Sometimes we seem to be praying to show God how
good, how faithful, how dedicated we are. We put in
time to win some kind of "grace" that may have nothing
to do with any kind of personal relationship with God or
anyone else. Prayer becomes a quid pro quo bargaining
arrangement in which we say: " Well, I did my part, gave
you my precious time, God, now you do something."

The deepest motivation for prayer is that we want and
need God to love us with a love that can transform us. I
go to eucharist to praise and thank God, surely, but I also
gather with a community, listen to God's word, and
receive eucharist, so that all of these can transform me. I
can become the body of Christ with whom I gather and

that I receive. I hear a word that consoles or challenges or teases me to a new insight or activity. I sit with scripture, pondering it in the quiet of my room so that this word can be a transforming word.

Prayer is asking God to love us, letting that love transform us, so that, eventually, we will be filled with the fire of God's Spirit and we will renew the face of the earth. At one time we were encouraged to say the rosary so that Russia could be converted. Superficially that seemed to mean that if we prayed the rosary often and sincerely enough God, who otherwise did not much care what happened to Russians, would swoop down and make them change from atheists to believers, from the red menace to orthodox lambs. Still, there was a wisdom in the notion. I sincerely believe that if all American Catholics did say the rosary, ponder the mysteries of Christ's life, unite ourselves with the "be it done" of Mary, our entire population would be so transformed that the entire world would be renewed, converting Russia, and everyone else.

## Prayer Is Getting the Questions Right

I detest the bumper sticker: "Jesus is the answer." It appears to me far more true that Jesus is the one who helps us live with the questions. Many times, Jesus himself is the question or at least reframes the question for us. I came to this realization once as I was speaking at a Religious Education Congress. I said something unplanned. I stopped. I asked someone to write my words down and tell me later what I had said. A person in the audience that day made me a poster showing a father holding his child in his arms as he gazed at the ocean on a lovely sunny day. Underneath the picture were my words:

"We ask God for answers, and God gives us a person to help us live with the question."

We want to know the answers to all life's mysteries and God sends us Jesus to walk alongside us in the midst of ambiguity, doubt, uncertainty, real life. Oftentimes Jesus comes in the form and face of another, a brother, a sister who is with us through our various questionings, not providing premature or easy solutions, but waiting with us for truth to evolve in its own time and its own way. We have an enduring "lust for certitude," as Sam Keen once said. Something in the human psyche desperately wants to know the exact truth, without ambiguity or mystery. But that is not the world God created, not the world we inhabit. Paradoxically, it was Sam Keen, working with James Fowler on the development of faith through various stages, who has helped us see this lust for certitude as a rather primitive faith. Their portrait of faith from the primitive, initial faith of the child to that of the adult suggests that maturity demands the ability to live with ambiguity. The need to have every question answered, every mystery solved characterizes the immaturity of one who has not developed a personal, integrated, interiorized belief. Faith, and the prayer that underlies it, depends more on getting the questions right than on having the answers.

In the midst of enormous controversy in our archdiocese a few years ago I was told about the priest who began mass praying: "In the name of the Father, Son, and Holy Spirit, *and nobody else.*" He wisely refused to trust completely anyone but God, and to retain uncertainty in areas which will always remain uncertain.

As a priest, I hear too often the damage done by those who are too sure, who *know* what others should do or be, or believe. "My mind is made up, don't confuse me

with the facts." When I am asked to help people pray, I
need the charism to encourage people to wait, to hold
on, to act with courage even in the face of too little
knowledge, too many questions, too few answers. I must
be like Elie Wiesel's rabbi who told him when he was a
little boy, "I pray to get the questions right." We pray so
that we will know what the questions are, and how the
questions best are framed.

## Prayer is a radical response to life

This definition of prayer is stolen from Matthew Fox's
*On Becoming a Musical Mystical Bear.* Each word of
the definition is important, but I will not spend much
time on all of them now. Already I have tried to make the
point in many ways that prayer is rooted in our life, in
real life, in life as it is, not as we would like it to be.

Also, prayer is relational, a response within a relationship. My entire subtext throughout these pages reflects
on our relationship with, and our response to God.
Prayer is central to this relationship. I cannot see the
face of God unless it is I who sees it. I need to be present. It is not enough to be physically at eucharist, or in
prayer. I need to be there emotionally, consciously. Over
and over in *The Spiritual Exercises,* St. Ignatius wisely
suggests that the retreatant ask for the grace he or she
wants. We need to know what we are searching for or
we cannot see it when it comes. We need to name how
we want God to respond if we are to recognize the
response. More concretely, I need to pay attention to my
heart, my desires, my questions, my longings if my
prayer is to be real. My closest friend, Sharon, asks me
often, "Pat, how's your heart?" If she doesn't ask, I am in
danger of not knowing. God asks the same thing:
"Where are you? What is going on in your life? What are

your fondest hopes, your deepest dreams, your most secret longings?"

I heard a priest recently speak about celibate sexuality. He was frank, honest, genuine. His opening words were: "I'm too old to lie anymore." That human stance makes prayer possible. I cannot meet God, or anyone else unless I am there without deceit, dishonesty or pretense.

The final dimension of prayer in the above definition (prayer as radical response to life) requires some reflection if we are to truly find God in that prayer. Prayer is radical in the sense that if I pray, if I see the face of Christ, if I meet God, it will get at the roots of my life. I will be uprooted, re-rooted: I will be changed, con-verted, turned around. Prayer, precisely because it is rela-tional, personal, and involved with my real life is trans-forming. If I pray, I, not God will be changed. In a very real sense, the test of prayer's validity always entails the questions: "Did it matter? Did I change? Was the world at all disrupted because God entered it again?"

Prayer, whether personal or communal/liturgical, ought to be disruptive in our lives. At St. Leo we often pray the Lord's prayer, "Our Mother, Our Father who art in heaven...." I preface this prayer with words like: "Let us pray in the way that Jesus taught us to pray." Often a visitor or someone who notices the change for the first time will ask why we add "Our Mother" to the way Jesus prayed. My response is to suggest that if we are truly to pray *the way* Jesus prayed we need to use different words, because that is what he did. Jesus prayed in a way that shocked his contemporaries. "When you pray," he seemed to say, "call God 'Daddy,' or 'Pop.'" He said this to a people who did not even pronounce Yahweh, the name of God, to a people who kept God remote, dis-tant and unnameable. Jesus invited people into a famil-iarity with a God who was like a dear, intimate family member. To capture the same shock, we do well to pray "our Mother." We need to pray in some fashion that takes us out of too easily speaking of, or with, God, as if we knew who and how God is.

Prayer changes us. It gives us the courage to make changes. I have directed significant retreats in which the retreatant finally decided to get divorced or leave the priesthood. Honesty, reality, intimacy with God often afford the courage to make difficult choices others will not approve or understand.

Some years ago, before the Vatican saw fit to investigate his ministry, Archbishop Raymond Hunthausen of Seattle illustrated for me the transforming power of prayer, its radicalizing dimension. During two successive Lents and one intervening Advent, he wrote to the members of the archdiocese inviting us to bring to our prayer the reality of where we lived. The Seattle archdiocese is coextensive with the largest military constellation in the country, surrounded by McChord Air Force Base, the enormous Fort Lewis complex, a nuclear submarine facility at Bangor, the Naval shipyard in Bremerton, and various other smaller military presences. Our largest single employer in the region is Boeing, a gigantic military contractor. Conscious of all of this, Archbishop Hunthausen wrote a letter to everyone in the archdiocese, suggesting that we pray about our response to this reality: What did it mean to be a follower of Jesus in the Puget Sound area just before the launching of the first Trident submarine, the most powerful destructive weapon in the history of the world? We were asked to prayerfully ponder this question in Lent, in Advent, then in Lent again. Not long after the second Lent, on the vigil of Pentecost, the archbishop spoke at Pacific Lutheran University. He reflected on the threat of nuclear holocaust emanating largely from our own area of the world. He very tentatively suggested that it might make sense for believing Christians to withhold that portion of our income tax that goes to military spending. This suggestion received enormous publicity, though it was only a small portion of a wonderful, challenging speech. Because of the publicity and the obvious chord he touched, the archbishop personally decided to withhold that portion of his income tax, breaking the law and risking certain fines and possible imprisonment.

At no time did the archbishop suggest what anyone else ought to do. At no time did he invite anyone else to do anything but pray. Whether or not any of the rest of us did indeed pray is questionable, but obviously Archbishop Hunthausen took his own advice, prayed, and was moved to action quite relevant to the incarnational situation in which he and we exist. His prayer was also rooted in place, as he visited the naval base, and prayed there with others. This prayer transformed him, radicalized him. The cost of that decision became all too clear when the painful investigation that disrupted his ministry and the life of our entire archdiocese occurred. No one seriously doubts that the real reason for the right-wing attacks on his ministry flowed much more from his anti-military activism than from so-called liturgical abuses easily found in many, if not most, dioceses.

This issue created the largest volume of letters to the editor I have ever seen. Secular papers throughout the region and our diocesan paper were inundated with mail, most of it derogatory, about the archbishop's decision. The one that most struck me and is most germane to this discussion came from a military officer suggesting that, by taking this stance of protest and political action, the archbishop had given up on the power of prayer and turned to secular rather than spiritual means. This sadly too typical letter witnesses to an heretical desire to disconnect prayer from life. We would be more comfortable if prayer did not disturb us but, rather, forced God to change so that we need not. Archbishop Hunthausen believed that because he risked praying he had to be faithful to where that prayer led him, whatever anyone else might be called to do, or not do.

I appreciated this concept of prayer as radical and dangerous, leading us to places we might rather not be, through the experience of a woman who is now a staff member at our parish. She had made *The Spiritual Exercises in Everyday Life*. Her "election" in the midst of the retreat was, in her own words, "to get a life." A single woman in her mid-thirties, she very shortly thereafter took a foster daughter into her home, and has struggled with enormous joy over the past three years to incorporate responsible motherhood into her work life in the church. She would affirm that decision which came precisely out of prayer as the best she ever made, but also the most difficult and most life-disrupting.

*Synthesis*

Finally, in this reflection on prayer let me tie some things together. Prayer radicalizes us, but it does so within the context of our specific lives. I was teaching a class in Spiritual Direction once. While reflecting on the radical dimension of prayer I was very conscious of the presence in class of a woman who had begun the Peace and Justice center in Spokane, Washington. She had a marvelous history of involvement in social issues and causes relative to our lives of faith. I felt marginally ungenuine as I spoke, as if with authority, on a subject on which she was expert. Toward the end of class she raised her hand and said something very moving and enlightening to me. She directly complimented me on the consistency of what I was saying with the way she saw me living my life. She thanked me for being outspoken in support of women's ministry in the church, for excellent collaboration with lay ministers, for my defense of those not ordained in the Catholic Church. I had never previously considered my support for women as "action on behalf of justice," nor seen this rather natural stance as the outgrowth of transforming prayer. It had been relatively easy for me to take such a stance because it flowed directly from the events of my life. However, this woman was right. The circumstances of my life had led me, if I was to be honest, to a radical position in the area of lay ministry, women's rights, a declericalization of the church. I often felt guilty about other causes to which I had not responded, issues I had not been involved in, actions I had not taken. But this respect for feminism, and the gifts of women in and for the church, flowed directly from my life, my ministry and my prayer. We need not look for the areas of injustice that we need to address. They stare us in the face if we but look. That is true for me and for each one of us.

I often felt guilty when I thought of Jean Vanier (the founder of L 'Arche, an international community of people with handicapping conditions and those choosing to live with them). Vanier truly lives the gospel. Similarly, I felt guilty thinking of Mother Teresa. My hope was that when Mother Teresa thinks of Jean she feels guilty and when Jean Vanier thinks of Mother Teresa, he feels guilty too! I had the chance to ask Jean once if I was correct. He admitted that he did feel inadequate and a bit guilty when he thought of the heroic sanctity of Mother Teresa. We all are tempted to think we should be doing what someone else does, without appreciating the path along which God leads us in prayer and in life.

I believe we find God in prayer, or more accurately,

that God finds us. Prayer happens when we let our relationship with God be real, rooted in our individual and unique lives. Prayer happens when we do not decide ahead of time where the sacred places, the sanctuaries, and temples lie, but let God lead us to them. Prayer happens when we are willing to let the questions be and do not hurry to find solutions. Prayer happens when we let God love us where and how we actually are. Prayer happens when we let the word of God invite us into its moods, its manifestations, its wonder, and live the mystery, making it our own, not as an old story, but as one transforming us right now. If we pray, each of us will put on a different face of Jesus, each of us will become a quite different incarnation of God's love.

Much of our prayer takes place in the midst of a community, within the church, yet the church itself can be so problematic, so let me turn to the struggle to find God within the church.

# 3.

## Christ's Fragile Body:
## Finding God in the Church

*Living the truth in love, we should grow in every*
*way into him who is the head, Christ, from whom*
*the whole body, joined and held together by every*
*supporting ligament, with the proper functioning*
*of each part, brings about the body's growth and*
*builds itself up in love* (Eph 4:14-6).

Within this chapter I hope to help us grow into
Christ, reflecting some on the proper functioning
of the various parts, including ourselves, which make up
the body of Christ. Again, I want to do so through experiences that touch us, reminding us of where we find
God, and sadly in the case of the church, where we may
not. As with the past two chapters, let me begin with an
experience of prayer.

Today as you enter into a moment of quiet, I invite you
to picture your parish, your church, your local community, wherever, and whoever it is with whom you worship.
Perhaps you will want to let your memory return to a
church in which you were at home, and felt comfortable. I invite you to remember some occurrence of experiencing God, of finding Christ, of tasting their Spirit
within that community.

Perhaps you will recall a funeral you attended that was especially comforting, consoling.

Or a wedding where people who were really part of that community, promised to be a sign of Christ's presence to each other and to all...

A Sunday mass on some special occasion that really "worked..."

The baptism of a child who was part of your life, in which this community truly embraced the child and its parents and promised to be with them. . .

An Easter vigil...

A particular song that captures this community's spirit and flavor...

A sacred window, or other artifact that speaks God to you...

Where has God been present? Where has Christ been authentically alive, however momentarily? Where has the breath of the Spirit blown over you?

Stay with that memory for a few moments, being grateful, perhaps wondering why or how this presence occurred.

Once again, this moment of reflection may well be the best part of the chapter, but allow me to interrupt in order to tell you the remembrance that comes to me as I enter into a similar exercise. I need to take some time to tell the story. It combines everything I have to say about finding God in the church.


## AN EXPERIENCE OF CHURCH

The event was Clarence Williams' funeral. To appreciate the funeral, I have to tell you about Clarence, a large, simple African-American, a Vietnam veteran with some woundedness in his brain and in his heart. Clarence joined our community through the catechumenate five years ago. For several years before that Clarence was on the edge of the community. He was visible as the almost daily companion of a widow in the neighborhood. Diminutive Kathy, in her late sixties, Clarence more than twice her size, and her dog were frequently seen walking all around our dangerous Hilltop neighborhood. Clarence was a bodyguard of sorts, but also a friend. They made a strange sight, this burly, quiet man, and the effervescent widow, and so were recognized in every part of the area.

Clarence had also been on the edge of the community because he worked as a maintenance person for the Vocation-Technical school adjacent to the church. He told us later that he used to eat his lunch on the roof of the school, watching to see if it was safe to come over. He wondered, curious whether we were who we pretended to be—a real church, not the phony ones he had seen all his life. Clarence saw the hungry being fed, the sick cared for, families being given baskets of food. He saw men and women of different colors, shapes and sizes. He saw people coming into the church to pray privately or to attend services. He had even seen his friend Kathy go there. He watched, and eventually came to church to see for himself.

For many weeks he stood around the back, not even entering the church proper, until he finally came in and stayed. He asked about joining, was told about our RCIA (Rite of Christian Initiation of Adults) process, was invited, and began to attend. For many weeks he said nothing, not even responding as the group took turns sharing something of their faith and life. Still, he seemed intent on joining. When he did speak it was always curt, sometimes gruff. The RCIA director found him difficult to fathom. Still Clarence kept coming. There was some-

thing in his large, hulking presence that did not frighten
but gave peace.

Slowly, Clarence began to talk, to tell his story, to
share his pain-filled life. He offered his insights and per-
ceptions of reality, often exactly on the mark. Slowly
Clarence became the heart of the group. He was excited
at the prospect of being baptized. Frequently as the
Easter Triduum approached, we found him in the church
looking at our horse-trough-like baptismal tub, wondering if he would fit. He barely did. At the Easter vigil we
had to bend Clarence sideways almost stuffing him into
the tub, but under he went, emerging with the most glo-
rious, beatific smile imaginable. He stood in the waters
as the community sang, tears running down his face; we
almost had to force him to get out for the next person.

The year that Clarence was baptized the neophytes
(those just baptized) wore their white robes throughout
the Easter season at every mass they attended. Clarence
wore his with enormous pride, going to almost every
mass that Easter season, sometimes three a weekend. I
will never forget the sight of Clarence, with his Levis and
T-shirt beneath the white robe that reached barely to his
knees and stretched tight across his massive chest. One
Sunday a week or two after Easter, an usher failed to
show up. At the last minute someone grabbed Clarence,
still standing in the back in his white robe and asked
him to help. Given no clear instructions, Clarence took
the collection basket and roared around the church,
putting the basket under every chin, shaking it somewhat insistently. As far as he knew, the initial request
constituted a permanent appointment, so for the remain-
ing weeks of the Easter season Clarence took up the collection. My dominant impression of him will forever be
in his white robe, wandering around the church with no
apparent plan or order, collecting money. I suspect we

lost a lot of income by that randomness, but the good will built up more than covered any loss.

Over the next months Clarence gradually became a part of the parish. He was present at most events, helped where he could, spoke little, but smiled often. He worked for a while in a nursing home but lost the job because he spent too much time chatting with the elderly patients. One of our staff helped Clarence learn to drive so he could get a job delivering packages.

Then, suddenly, just a year after that Easter, at thirty-eight, Clarence was dead. After a summer evening Saturday mass, someone rushed up to me and told me to go to Clarence's apartment where he was lying unconscious. I arrived to discover the body already lifeless on the floor, in a spartan apartment with a table, a chair, a TV set, a newspaper and a Bible, perhaps a single change of clothes. I anointed his body. His dear friend Kathy, the one of so many walks together, had found him. Apparently he had an asthma attack, choked and died rather abruptly, for Kathy had seen him just thirty minutes earlier.

All of this narrative leads up to the funeral. We could find no family, no friends except those made at church. One of the staff had heard Clarence say he had a family once, but had lost track of them. When we held the funeral one evening about three hundred parishioners came. Had Clarence died a year earlier, perhaps only Kathy would have been there, but now he had a home, a family, people who loved him, and for whom he had quickly become significantly special. This was the church, Christ's body, his friends. Because the parish was his family, we all gathered in the vestibule to meet and greet and bless the body. We stood around the simple casket singing *Amazing Grace*, and entered with Clarence as the song continued.

The homily was rooted in the readings from Easter, consisting of memories from members of the community telling their favorite stories of Clarence. The wife of the man who had been his sponsor for baptism told two stories. The first occurred the day she met Clarence. Their family had invited him to dinner. When he arrived he barely said hello, walked right by the family in search of a TV room where he embedded himself, found a wrestling match and informed them to let him know when dinner was ready. The speaker said she remembered thinking, "It's going to be a long year!"

The second story occurred the day of the parish picnic just a few weeks before his death. Her family had accepted the responsibility for organizing the picnic and Clarence agreed to help. On a Sunday morning between our two masses, he loaded twenty tables and accompanying chairs onto a truck, and took them to a park where he carefully unloaded and set them up. Then it began to rain. Clarence loaded up the tables and chairs and put them back on the truck, brought them back to church, and was half-finished unloading them when the rain stopped. He began to load up again ready to take those chairs and tables back to the park. This stranger, now friend, so uncomfortable a few months before would now willingly, lovingly do anything for that family and for us.

That spirit of mutual dependence pervaded Clarence's funeral and our mourning. We laughed as much as we cried, consoled each other and trusted in Jesus whose resurrection was at the very center of our friendship with, and love for Clarence. He had become one of us at Easter and his funeral was a mass of resurrection, recalling and deepening that event. One who had had no home and no family before had found one in us. We were incredibly enriched by his presence, his faith, his now all-pervasive joy. With Clarence we had grown into him who is our head, Christ, and the body's growth had ineluctably been built up in love.

Clarence loved us, and we loved him. As we celebrated his passing and remembered him, we were all caught up into the depths of the Easter mystery so central to our shared faith. We had helped Clarence to believe in God, in himself, in humankind. Finally, he helped us to depend on, articulate and deepen the faith into which we had welcomed him.

The story of this relationship we had with Clarence, and this celebration of his death, constitute for me everything I would want to say about church. Here, for a moment, we the church were who we say we are, who we want to be—a community, loving, welcoming, supporting. Here the face of Christ was seen, felt, touched, tasted. We could all believe in the Christ who binds us together in love. We experienced ourselves as the body of Christ. This is the church in which I deeply believe, to which I am forever bonded and into which I invite others.

## THE PROBLEM OF CHURCH

I start with this so wonderful, so positive story because I share with many others a central problem. I deeply believe in Jesus. I even deeply love being a priest. Still, the church drives me crazy, makes me crazy. The issues at which I bristle may be mine, not yours, but I need to acknowledge them, need to be honest with you and with myself. I need to see the incredible importance of Clarence, and others like him, if faith is to remain alive in me or anyone else. If you do not struggle with the church, if you do not find it difficult to believe in the church, I suspect you have friends or children or spouses who do. It is important to understand them. Personally, like the priest I mentioned earlier, I am too old to lie anymore. I need to admit that the church I love and serve has an almost unfathomable capacity to hurt people. I have struggled with the evidence of that hurt all my adult life.

I write as an ordained minister of the Roman Catholic Church, which I love, yet which manages to make me crazy. I know from many friends, ordained and lay alike, in other denominations of the Christian Church that we are not alone. Our shortcomings are different in kind but similar in quality to other religious bodies. I cannot speak from others' experiences but suspect that theirs will resonate with mine. All institutions are somewhat alike.

Institutions have a power in people's lives that can be frightening. Throughout my priestly life, I have witnessed the negative impact of that power. Among all institutions, the church, because of its relationship with God, and all that we hope from it and expect for it, has an especially great power to hurt. Throughout my priestly life I have listened to the stories of people trying to match their honest experience of what it means to be sexual with what their church tells them about sexuality. I have heard the pain of a family trying to trust their own experience of sexuality and marriage, being told that their behavior is at odds with the church, in fact, with God's will for them. I have had gay and lesbian friends told that they were inherently evil, and that any expression of who they are in an act of love is always seriously evil.

I know that for the past ten years there has been a hole in my life, a kind of enduring ache because I live and minister within the Archdiocese of Seattle. I experienced with so many others an entirely tangible suffering when the church he served so publicly attacked the ministry of Archbishop Raymond Hunthausen, the finest follower of Jesus I have ever known well. This ideal bishop, a gentle, quiet man who loves people and trusts God, who empowers others with the grace of the gospel, this man who lives that gospel himself to his very toenails was formally investigated, then told he was not adequate as a bishop and another must take over his ministry. This investigation, especially in its secrecy and its dishonesty, was immensely disillusioning to me and to many all around me. We went through a collective purgatory. "If this man," we seemed to feel, "is not living the gospel of Jesus then we do not know how to do it." The archbishop handled it better than most of us. I recall him reflecting early in the investigating process that the worst thing that could happen would be for Rome to tell him he could not be bishop anymore and would have to go back to Montana and go fishing! The rest of us, especially those working most closely with the church, experienced enormous struggle and tension between institutional preservation and the lives and loves of people. It would be impossible to exaggerate the extent of the pain we in the Seattle area felt with regard to the church during those five or six years. I share this because it is true, it is "there," and it remains part of the difficulty in finding God, seeing the face of Christ, in the church, for myself and for many others.

I have also felt the pain of being a public minister of the church in the midst of our institutional sexism. I have worked with extremely talented women, many of them close friends, in a church that desperately needs ministers. That same church tells immensely talented women that they may not use the full extent of their gifts.

Once I was having dinner in my home with a group of

friends. A young seminarian was present. He demonstrated an almost pathological inability to share anything of
his own beliefs with others. One of the diners was a
close friend and coworker, a woman who had worked in
the church for fifteen years. She had an advanced degree
in psychology, a fine degree in theology, and years of
educational, pastoral experience. As we sat at dinner, we
struggled to discover what this seminarian who was to
be ordained in just six months believed or wanted to
pass on. We asked questions, gently probing till we
encountered his naive, but unacknowledged, all-but-total
lack of experience. Suddenly, the woman arose from
table and went to the back yard. I went to see what was
the matter and found her crying. She said, simply,
through tears, "What kind of church would ordain him,
and not me?"

I worked for seven years with a woman who is now
the "pastor" of a parish in Seattle. She describes her ministry as being given all the responsibility of any pastor,
yet being asked to work with one hand tied behind her
back. There are so many things she cannot do, things for
which she must get others, men/priests to do for her and
for her community, services she could perform perfectly
well herself if empowered to do so.

Yet the real source of pain around this issue for myself
and most people struggling to believe in the church concerns not just women getting power or position or pres-
tige (like I have, sadly). Much more significant and lam-
entable is the lack of access to the eucharist experienced
by so many Catholics, as well as the abysmally celebrated
masses and other rituals of the church to which so many
people are subjected. What is so painful in the church
today, almost to the point of incredulity, is our failure to
afford the sacramental life of Christ to people at the
same time that we say these sacraments are the very

source and substance of our lives. An eighty-five-year-old sister who visits the sick in our parish, and has walked with hundreds of dying people cannot anoint them. As the only priest I am often unable to visit them frequently, perhaps even in a critical moment. When I do, I sometimes do not know them. A professional counselor on our parish staff, teaches, and touches and heals people day after day after day, yet she cannot offer the church's formal sacrament of reconciliation. In so many parishes, a team of people prepares couples for marriage, another individual tests and counsels them, a third person prepares the ritual, and leads them through the rehearsal, and then a priest whom they have scarcely met, hurried and harried and perhaps performing his third wedding of the weekend, celebrates the ceremony with them. The church continues to hurt people, sometimes to inhibit the very faith we want to convey through the paucity, scarcity, or insincerity of the services we are able to offer because of our circumscription of who can lead the celebration, limiting it to unmarried men.

I find myself increasingly concerned, not just with the limitations placed on women or married men who feel called to leadership in our church, but also with the lack of honesty about the history and practice of celibacy in order to maintain the present position. A growing body of literature suggests the numbers of women and even men who have been hurt by good priests unable to live up to the standards set for them. The lack of choice regarding whether a priest be celibate or married minimizes the witness of those who choose to, and then actually live, in a celibate way.

In honesty, the deepest pain that I experience as a priest in a life I deeply love, is that each time I am who I am, I hurt people too. I represent, in the very ministry I love, a structure that is dysfunctional and exclusionary, limiting who is served and who can serve. It is painful to know each time I celebrate eucharist, or preach, however well I do so, I am part of the process of pain to many women, or married men who experience the same call to ministry, a call not officially acknowledged today in the church. The priesthood would not be helped significantly by my absence, and so I will continue, but it hurts deeply to know that I am part of the pain for others.

Sadly, I could continue with the disbelief engendered by the church, but I suspect I have gone on enough to capture the idea. In its institutional manifestation, the church is at least as able to destroy as it is to foster faith.

### ALTERNATE MODELS OF CHURCH

But the church is not exclusively or even primarily an institution. Vatican II, speaking of the church, begins with the insistence that the church is a mystery, specifically the mystery of the people of God. A mystery, technically, is not something we cannot understand at all, but rather something we will never understand completely. We can come to know a lot, but never everything. What that means, in part, is that we do not fully know who we are. We are always in need of reformation on our way to becoming what we are called to be.

Avery Dulles urged us some years ago in *Models of the Church,* to acknowledge that the church, besides being an *Institution* is also *Community, Herald, Servant, Sacrament.* The church would no longer exist if it did not have some structure, some authority (always open to abuse), some parameters of action, behavior, ritual, etc. But the church also would fail to exist if as a body we did not try to become a *community*, a gathering of people who love one another as we have been loved. The church would not exist if it did not continue to proclaim (herald) that "Jesus is Lord," preaching that message in season and out. The church would no longer exist if followers of Jesus were not laying down their lives for their friends, serving the needs of the poor, giving unstintingly of time and talent to those within and without the body. The church would no longer exist if it were not a sign in the world of the presence of Christ, bringing about what it signifies by that very presence, that sacramental presence. The church is institutional, and like any institution it can hurt, manipulate, control, and abuse people by the very structure that was intended to save. I am not so naive as to believe that we human beings can exist without institutions, nor that any institution will ever live up to the dream with which it began. Still, to find God, to see the face of Christ, while acknowledging the hurt, to continue to affirm the presence of the Spirit in our midst, I know that I need continuously to look more broadly. I need to remember Clarence and the community that welcomed him, the servant he became, the message he heard and proclaimed, the sign he was of God's presence in the world.

## THINGS I HAVE LEARNED ABOUT THE CHURCH

I need to remember and reflect on how I have seen the face of Jesus, in so many ways in the church, to treasure those memories, to be able to build a life on them. Let me share some other things I have learned about the church that help me to believe.

*What faith I have comes from the very church that so often disturbs me*

The church that makes me crazy is this very church from which Archbishop Hunthausen drew his faith, and

draws it still. Within this church that upsets me my
mother and father learned to believe and passed that
faith on to me. I believe in large part because of the faith
passed on to me from the representatives of the institution and my family. Though I smile at some of the things
we did as church while my parents were leading me to
faith, at the time they fed me fully. I recall my father
teaching my brother and myself to say the Morning
Offering. Each day for an entire summer he left notes
somewhere for us to find, usually before noon, reminding us to say "The Big MO." One morning my toothbrush
had a note wrapped around it; another day the note was
in my shoe. Once I found it as I went to get a golf ball
out of my bag. Each day a reminder, and eventually a
habit, a sharing in the devotional life of the church.
However much my life of prayer might change, I still
believe it not a bad idea at all to offer my "joys, hopes
and sufferings" each day to God, for the good of the people we call church. At my Father's funeral my brother,
again by his own accounting not a terribly religious person, insisted on saying the Morning Offering as a way of
remembering our Father who was, whatever faults were
his, inarguably a man of the church.

### *The church is not supposed to "work"*

It has taken me twenty years to learn this, but I have
come to understand that brokenness is the whole point.
Getting along with each other is our very reason for existence. If it were easy to get along with one another Jesus
would not have talked about it so much. I used to think it
was an aberration that so much emotional, spiritual, psy-
chological energy was expended just getting along with
the very people with whom we expected to work. For
years, as a professional church person I resented the

infighting, the politicizing, the intramural wars that always occurred. Early in my priesthood I was all but destroyed by being in the center of an ideological battle over the direction of a school. Certainly the tensions were as much my own fault as anyone's, but I could not imagine why we who professed to follow Jesus, who were all responding to the Call of the King, could not get along, agree to disagree and support each other.

Now it seems to me that the very point of our faith, the reason for the existence of the church as a community of the fragile followers of Jesus, is that it is very difficult for people to agree, to get along and to manage to love each other no matter what. The church exists to be a sign that this is possible. The church is like dancing in a circle; we never get anywhere, and we keep bumping into each other. When it is all over what will matter will not be the tasks we get done, the work we perform, but the quality of our love relationships with each other.

A great, prophetic Jesuit who has worked for most of the past twenty-five years in our neighborhood has primarily taught me this important lesson. Out of deep concern for the poor, and a passion for justice, this dedicated, yet somehow playful priest has undertaken a hundred different projects, started fifty programs, invited literally hundreds of people to join with him. By his own admission, nothing he has ever done has "worked." All of the problems he has addressed—hunger, homelessness, care for the mentally ill, substance abuse, military expenditures in the face of poverty—all have gotten worse, not better. He insists it does not matter because what matters is the quality of the relationships of the people doing them, whether or not the project changes the world, or any part of it. He extends to the communal level that famous anonymous dictum that we do not engage in social action in order to change the world, but so that the world will not be able to change us.

This realization leads me, now, to spend a great deal of time, in collaborative ministry, in staff meetings, in shared prayer, shared life, in retreats and planning days and play days with those with whom I work. Because what finally matters is not what we get accomplished, but how we get along with one another while we are trying to accomplish it. *The process, not the product, is the point!* The church in a deep sense is not supposed to work. Getting things done has nothing to do with being the community of Jesus; loving each other does. When we are finally successful, we will be finished, and the *parousia* will have arrived.

### *The chosen people are not so hot*

I learned this in dialogue with a catechumen in our parish in my second year at St. Leo. Kerry is a doctor, trained to be skeptical about non-scientific, spiritual, religious matters. He has always been a caring, loving person, the kind of doctor not at all concerned with making money, who volunteers at every clinic in town, who gives himself unstintingly to his patients and especially to the poor. He came to our RCIA process because his wife, a Catholic, asked him to at least look at her faith. He entered filled with cynicism, questioning everything, not easily led to simple answers, or comfortable belief. In the course of the year, Kerry began to come to mass with his wife. It made him angry. He liked it. He and his wife sat behind the L'Arche community, a group of seven or eight people with handicapping conditions, and people who lived with them.

Over time Kerry was especially captivated by Bill, an aging man with Down syndrome, whose smile, wit, charm and warmth are truly infectious. He even became Bill's physician. Kerry kept coming to the RCIA because, as he said: "No one can sit behind Bill Downey week after week and not believe in God." This did not remove his skepticism concerning the church. He was very challenging, forcing anyone who taught within the process to be very careful what we said, what we asserted to be true. He came every week with his "guns loaded," looking for an excuse not to finally join us. I remember vividly one session in which, somewhat out of the blue, Kerry asked "What is this B. . . S . . . about the 'chosen people?' Who do you think you are to call yourselves chosen, somehow better than others?" Apparently he had listened to the preface at mass the previous weekend and heard the phrase: "You are a chosen race, a royal priesthood, a people set apart."

It was a very good question, asked as if to say, "All right Carroll, I've got you now." In a moment of grace, a response, not an answer, came to me, though I was not leading the group. I have come to appreciate this response more now than when it first crossed my lips. I suggested that historically God chose the Hebrew people not because they were the brightest and the best, but because they were the weakest and the worst. God calls, chooses and invites communities and individuals not because they are so great, but because they so need to be loved and cherished. If our Judeo-Christian history is to be trusted, those specially chosen are the neediest of all, people like myself and him. Kerry's response was a wonderfully, muted "Damn you!"

My point was and is that he and we can live with and believe in a church that is built on fragility, weakness, inadequacy. He had no trouble with Marx's critique of religion as providing a "crutch." We are all, indeed, a bit crippled. Kerry's faith grew and blossomed because of the most fragile yet most important person in our community. His faith could flourish if it meant that he was called to baptism out of weakness, not strength.

I recall with special delight, Kerry's baptism at the Easter vigil that year. Having come kicking and screaming, resisting as best he could every inch of the way, he knelt in that font, looked at the baptizing deacon and said, loudly enough for all the church to hear, "All the way, Tom!" The deacon pushed him almost violently under the water three times, drenching him in the name of Father, Son and Holy Spirit, splashing water in all directions, saturating the altar space, and wiping out the holy oils we were to use for confirmation later. The congregation, many of whom knew his struggle to reach that moment, stood and applauded, sharing his enormous joy. This entire episode helped me as none other to look at the church and believe because of weakness, fragility, ineptitude, trusting that the church is credible not because it is so good, but because it and we are so needy.

### We need to see with the eyes of those entering or coming back

I have learned that we long-time perhaps jaded Catholics can profitably adjust our vision. One of the recent joys of parish life has been the rediscovery of the *Rite of Penitents*. The name is not as helpful as the idea, which is to celebrate ritually the return of former Catholics to the table. We, like many parishes, offer a program called "ReMembering Church," in which we try to offer the opportunity to put the members back together with the body. Those who decide to formally rejoin are ritually welcomed through the lenten season, being the first to receive the ashes on Ash Wednesday, the first to receive eucharist on Holy Thursday, and are prayed for throughout the intervening season. It is a painful process, but a richly rewarding one. Often the struggles of inactive Catholics touch on how a priest or teacher treated them or a member of their family. I find myself continually apologizing for the hurts and pains inflicted. More positively though, my faith is nourished when I hear why others come back, what they feel, what touches them, that we might not notice otherwise.

Toward the end of our time together a year ago, we asked those sharing in the rites of Lent: "Why did you come back? What moved you? Why did you come? Why do you stay? What is it that allows you to believe within this church community?"

One spoke of coming because he initially saw a community that was feeding people and we let him help, even though he had not been to church in a long time. He continued to experience being accepted as he was, on his own terms. He was not judged or criticized but loved as he was. Another spoke of coming to our Pentecost celebration, her first time in church in twelve years. An avowed feminist, she was overwhelmed at how "feminine" the service was in a church she judged to be so male-dominated; she spoke of colors, sounds, textures, incense, robes, graceful movements, softness, joy and warmth—qualities she had not expected to find, but continued to experience in today's church, where she now, often, is one of the dancers at major feasts.

Another woman, an animal psychologist for whales, who works in our local zoo, accidentally happened back for the same Pentecost celebration. She was not quite so taken. She found the dancing, the abundant music, the spirit of exuberance, quite foreign. There was something welcoming about it all, but it was not mass as she had known it in Hawaii years before. She probably never would have returned had not a long-time parishioner noticed her, somehow sensed both her newness to St. Leo and her discomfort, and said to her at the Kiss of Peace, "Don't worry, dear, it's not always like this!"

A marvelous story illustrates why another woman spoke of experiencing welcome and warmth, a friendliness she had not known elsewhere, or before in the church. Recently divorced, having lost pretty much everything, she was living in a downtown loft and starting a new life in a variety of ways. She had come to mass one morning for the first time in thirty-five years. She came a half-hour early by mistake. She watched a music group with guitars and drums and people dressed quite casually prepare for mass. She looked around for an organ, hoping this motley crew would leave before the service started. The wonderful wife of one of the ushers was there early and sat beside her. She asked the visitor whether she was new to St. Leo, then, whether she had been away from the church? The woman visitor said: "Yes." The parishioner asked: "How long?" She replied: "Thirty-five years!" "Oh," the friendly welcoming woman said, "Have you been sick?" The story is funny, but the woman who gradually worked her way back into the community was overwhelmed, first, that someone would talk to her in church, and, secondly, that the words were so compassionate, and finally so true. She had indeed been sick for a long time.

We frequently discover the beauty of the church in such little things, a word of greeting, a gesture, even an apparently foolish question, all the action of the body of Christ, welcoming the body of Christ. We who come often can miss the friendliness of our community and take it for granted because the change has been so gradual.

Our former parish council president, who almost

always comes to the sessions of Remembering Church, illustrated my point about looking at the church with different eyes. He responded to the question of why he keeps coming back to the group by saying, "I haven't been sure why I come. I do not need to be here. I have never really had the courage to leave the church, but I realize tonight that I keep coming here because others keep coming back to the church, telling me what they see. Somehow this keeps me within the church, changes the way I see what I have always seen." There is something important in long-time members of the Church needing to see through the eyes of those who come fresh and open to our midst, for they see what we have. They see the beauty and the wonder and the awesomeness and the light to which we may become too accustomed. They can miss the warts for the warmth, miss the foibles for the faith, the troubles for the truths. They help us look again.

## Not everything can be fixed

My ability to find God in church has been strengthened by the recognition that we cannot always fix either people or things. The sometimes miraculous presence of the L'Arche community in our midst has led me to this appreciation. I think especially of Greg, another young man who is developmentally disabled. Greg is a fixture in our parish. He was part of the original L'Arche home which started thirteen years ago on our block but has since moved. For years Greg came to St. Leo, though he was not a Catholic. Usually he stood at the door and welcomed people, always knowing them by name, even after absences of five or ten years. He always helped with religious education for children, sitting with our kids, and enjoying their lessons with them. One day,

Greg asked to join the church. Our inclination was to simply baptize him. He had been part of the community for so long. Still, Greg and his companions in L'Arche wanted him to go through the process, so he entered the catechumenate and spent the year as part of that community.

Among many moving moments that presence led to I recall especially one session during Lent in which Greg told, almost verbatim, the entire story of the woman at the well from John's gospel. This took a long, long time, with many *hems* and *haws* and pauses of up to a minute, but those present will never hear that gospel passage the same way again. Greg was baptized at the Easter vigil. Our community always responds to the baptism itself, but this Easter night, Greg was still standing in the midst of the community and the RCIA director asked him, "Greg, is it your desire to be baptized?" He responded, a loud if faltering, "Y.........y......yes!" The entire congregation stood and cheered as he approached the font and remained standing as he was immersed.

My point in this story is that all this love and affirmation, all this appreciation cannot "fix Greg." He is loved and he knows it, deeply cherished and rightly so, but he still lives with his disability. He still cannot learn many things. He is still moody, and sometimes difficult to be around. He still takes forever to say what it is he wants to say. We have to love him as he is, not to make him better. Greg's disability is simply more visible than many of our own. We all, individually and as a community, as a church, need to be loved as we are. All the love, all the time in the world will not "fix" Greg, nor most of the rest of us. The love certainly brings a security, a comfort, an ability to go on, but it must precede, and not depend on the fixing. I think this unconditional love, before the fixing, is essential in my attitude towards the church. I love this community not as something outside, apart, away from me, but as my family, my religious home, with all its fragility and faults.

## I need the Church

Despite its failings, there are times I could not go on without the church, without a believing community with whom I gather to pray, to hope, to celebrate, to weep. I discovered this again and anew in the midst of what we have called Desert Storm. In all its violence and ambiguity that war was endurable at all only because of the community in which I gathered to pray. Almost all of us saw no merit in the war, saw the use of force and violence over oil as incredibly destructive, cruel and cynical. However, some had children there, and almost all had someone they knew. As I mentioned before, military establishments practically surround Tacoma. At the beginning of the war, shortly before Lent, we began to sing, "Oh Healing River, send down your waters."

During Lent we put sand in our holy water fonts. We surrounded the dry baptismal font with sand. We tried to taste the dryness of the desert even in the always green Northwest. We moved through Lent together, praying that the "blood would be washed from off of the sand." Our singing and our prayers did not stop the war, nor take away the pain of that violence or our involvement in it, but we endured together. Despite all the foibles of the church as institution, that Lent reminded me forcibly again that I cannot live, cannot sustain hope, cannot face the broken world we inhabit together without a believing community, without eucharist, without the penitential seasons, and the hope of Easter. All of this led me to a most fruitful paschal season. I wrote the following poem for our Easter bulletin:

*Blessed are they who Mourn*

"Oh Healing River..."
All Lent we sang the waters down.
Prayed to wash, from sand, the blood
parched land to fertile valley,
water to our lips,
our lives,
our loves.

Prayed Baptism come,
anew for some,
again for all.

And now, today, at dawn
Water!
Healing, living, baptismal.

Tear filled tub!
Tears of war won, though victory vacuous,
of lives parched by pain,
of loves lost or lingering,
from hunger,
homelessness,
hallucinations...

Our tears, human tears, abundant tears,
Healing tears,
tears plunged into,
buried into,
dying into ...
Into Easter!

Jesus born again,
his amniotic fluid formed from tears,

his tears,
our tears.
Born (re-born) with Him,
We will cry again,
But we need never weep.

All of which helps me to say I cannot live without the church.

In Lent of 1992 our parish celebrated Ash Wednesday by inviting Native American Catholics, many of them parishioners, to come and celebrate with us. Because we were in the midst of the 500th anniversary of Columbus' arrival, and the European encroachment into their lives, during mass we made a public apology for the harm done to them, their land and their way of life. Representatives of the native community received the ashes first, then placed the ashes on the foreheads of the rest of us. After mass many of us walked five miles together to the grave of Chief Leschi, an early leader who stood alone against the first governor of the territory of Washington, refusing to yield his people's precious land and water rights, for which he was murdered by that governor. Only as a group could I have spoken, with others, the penitence I feel. Only with a believing community could we have made a statement to our native brothers and sisters that they could even begin to hear. There is much we cannot do without a church, a people.

*The church at its best still inspires me*

Finally in this experiential summary of what I have learned that helps me believe, I must in all honesty assert that *I believe in the church because of martyrs.* The sudden death of six Jesuits and two of their companions in l989 in El Salvador most recently brought this home. I have already spoken about the trauma of this event in my life as a Jesuit and as a person. It also deeply touches my life as a Catholic, a member of the church. Out of the faith tradition to which I struggle to be faithful, people are still inspired to give their lives and everything they have because of their belief in Jesus and their commitment to the values he invited us to live. The credibility of the church, again, despite all faults, is immeasurably strengthened by the continuing fact, throughout our two thousand year history, that some have found a truth that is ultimate, a truth worth laying down life for, a truth to die for, a truth, therefore, worth living for. Despite all the pains mentioned, and many more, I cannot not believe in this community of the followers of Jesus, this servant band, this herald's voice, this dim, but sometimes sacramental sign, indeed this institution.

## CONCLUSION

I end, with a *reflection*, a *story*, and a *prayer*. The *reflection* is simply that I can understand why some (especially today, women) leave the church or drift away. We are not all that we should be. We never live up to our promise, or our hope. The only authentic Christian, probably, was Jesus himself. I understand and sometimes share the pain that drives good people from us. I only know that I cannot go, for I find God and see the face of Christ in this community called church, at least often enough to keep me around. My experience may be quite different from another's, but I hope these reflections can help some to discover, in their own best moments, concrete, personal, life-giving, faith-filled reasons for staying.

The *story* I wish were my own, but I read it in the

paper one day. A priest was at a supermarket buying groceries, dressed in his clerical collar. A young woman came up to him, rather amazed, and asked: "Are you a minister or something?" He replied that, indeed he was. The young woman shook her head and told him, "Man, you guys need to get a different logo!'"

"A Logo?" he asked.

"Yeah, logo," she replied. "You know, that thing you wear with the guy hanging on the cross? It's turning people off! You need a different logo!"

The *prayer* is that I, that we, will be *always* able to find the only face of Jesus we are likely to see in this life, within the face of that always broken body, the face of the church. May the logo of a crucified savior more fittingly suit this people.

# 4.

## Finding God in the Poor

*I was hungry and you gave me food, I was thirsty
and you gave me drink, a stranger and you welcomed me, naked and you clothed me, ill and you
cared for me, in prison and you visited me* (Mt
25:35).

This chapter continues our search for God, "where
God may be found." I want to raise and reflect on the
question of finding God, and here more than ever, *finding the face of Christ* in the poor, where Jesus said he
would be, and could be discovered.

To begin with a moment of personal history, I am
from a relatively comfortable, upper-middle class,
Republican family. As a Jesuit I have always had whatever
I needed in terms of clothes and creature comforts. I
have never been economically poor. I have struggled to
internalize throughout my priestly life what it might
mean to have an "option for the poor," to stand on the
side of the poor, to learn from the poor. My success has
been limited, but the challenge endures. My present
parish ministry is enmeshed in material poverty, downtown, near the city-county court house, the jail. We are
surrounded by social service agencies that feed, house
and offer primary medical care to the people of an aver-
age sized American city. All of my adult life and these
past ten years in particular lead me to almost incessant

reflection on poverty and the gospel. I believe the seriousness of Jesus' promise that we will find him in the hungry, thirsty, imprisoned. I search still to know what that means. In this chapter I share with you some of the glimpses I have received so far.

As with the previous chapters, I begin by inviting you into a moment of meditation. I base this prayer on a powerful life-experience of a close and sensitive friend.

The cathedral in Mexico city, I am told, is a luxuriously beautiful yet ambiguous tourist attraction. Let us imagine that we have been told the same thing and go to visit this cathedral. As we stand in the square before an enormous elaborate church, we face not merely a church, but a massive dilemma. Between us and the church some thousand beggars crowd our path. We cannot get to the church without passing through this overwhelming galaxy of the poor. We cannot, in this prayer, as perhaps in real life, get to the place, the house, the presence of God without passing through the poor in some fashion. The path that we choose is the ground of our prayer. In this consideration, as in life, we have a multiplicity of options. Before we go on, pause and respond to the question, "Would you go to the church? And if so, how?"

## *I Won't Go*

We may choose *not* to go to the cathedral after all. It is too difficult, too painful, too challenging, too guilt-inducing to get to this particular church, this so concrete presence of God. We may choose not to go. "Doubtless," we say to ourselves, "there are other ways." One of the options in this prayer, as in life, is to suspect that God can be found elsewhere, by other means, in other places. One need not pass through the poor. Indeed one can surely find God without taking this par-

ticular route to this specific church, but, we must wonder, will whatever God we find elsewhere be the God of
Jesus, or only the constructed God of Televangelists, of a
"Christian" faith that promises only financial success and
comfort-filled life to those who believe?

## Ignore the Poor

We may choose simply to put down our heads, ignore
those between us and the cathedral, rush to the church
and enter untouched, unmoved, unscathed by the poverty that seemed to block our path. In this prayer moment
again, as in life, we may ignore the poor, and go to God
unbloody and unbowed. Again, the God discovered in
such a church may not be the God of Jesus, but a more
comfortable God of our own devices, a first-world
church, in self-contained, impenetrable suburbs, apart
from a large dimension of the pain of our world.

## Give Everything

We may choose a more generous approach, one that
seems heroic. We may give some small amounts to each
beggar as we pass, slowly but certainly emptying our
pockets and our hearts to the pleas of each person,
deserving or not. In this prayer, as in life, we may
choose to give a quarter here, a dollar there, and a bit of
our heart to each, until we have nothing left. We have
become one of the beggars; we have joined, by our own
choice, the ranks of the poor, entering into solidarity
with them. Forevermore we will see the world through
their eyes. Some, indeed, do make this choice, the
Dorothy Days, the Rutillo Grandes, the Mother Teresas of
our church, in every age, or, on a more temporary basis,
the thousands of Jesuit volunteers, or others who give a
year or two of service before getting on with their lives,

only to discover they can never again "get on" with business as usual. Clearly this emptying of self and being-
with is a legitimate, and holy choice, but, perhaps, not
the possible, desired, or divinely-willed choice for every
one of us.

## Pick My Beggar

We may decide to pick a single beggar, and make her
or him our own. We cannot take care of all of the poor,
cannot solve every problem, every ill of this square, or
of the world. But we can today, and each time we come
to this sacred place, try to become one with a single beggar, a single issue, a specific cause that forces us to
touch the poor. We can decide to enter into the suffering, the life and the story of one person or one group of
these hurting people, to see a bit of the world through
other eyes than our own. A legitimate, demanding path
to this church and to this God honestly looks for the face
of Jesus in one of the faces in need before us and tries to
respond as authentically as possible. We acknowledge
humbly that we cannot do everything, but we will do
something. We make choices to reduce an insurmount-
able problem into manageable units, ideally in areas that
touch most closely on our everyday lives, and begin to
respond as best we can to the chosen part.

I invite you to stay for a few moments with this consideration, one that has haunted me since I first attended to
it. What has been your approach to such a reality in the
past, in a single instance, or in the entirety of your life?
What would be your preferred response today? What
response does God seem to ask of you, expect from you?
I suspect you will discover that divine desire not in some
distant "should" or "ought" but deep in your own belly,

in your guts, in what you really want to do at your best and truest self.

Stay with this reflection for a few moments, then let me go on with my reflections on the simple, but all pervasive issue of finding Christ in the poor. Within the confines of this chapter, I desire simply to raise the question of whether or not we (and I honestly mean both you and me) do indeed find Jesus where he said he would be? Do we find him in those in our midst who are hungry, thirsty, naked, in prison, or are we more comfortable looking for him everywhere else?

I would add to the obvious parameters of this question the need to consider that we may discover the presence of Jesus in the poorest, most broken parts of ourselves. Perhaps to discover God we need individually and collectively to put "our clay foot forward," each acknowledging our personal poverty.

## THE TRUTH OF THE BEATITUDES

I would further ask whether the blessings Jesus promised do in fact ring true? Are the poor in Spirit, blessed, happy? Do the merciful honestly have mercy shown them? Are those who hunger and thirst for justice, those who are persecuted, those who are meek truly blessed, happy?

One day when I was praying about these words in preparation for preaching the gospel the following Sunday, I received a phone call from a woman seeking help. She was ill. Her husband had left her alone with her three children. She was about to lose her apartment. She was desperate. This woman was poor, sorrowing, persecuted, ill, in a very real prison only partly of her own making. I promise you she was not happy, was not feeling blessed. The following day, for our staff prayer, someone suggested that we walk slowly around our block, later sharing what we see. It is truly an amazing double-block. Social services abound, efforts to create beauty, a garden here, a well-pruned tree there. Still, the dominant impression is quite bleak. I walked that morning aware of the hundred or so people of the streets, mostly men, waiting in the cold outside our kitchen which would open at 9:00. They had to leave the shelters at 7:00, and the Hospitality Kitchen would be their next stop. Hungry, cold and often angry, they were not happy.

On that same block there is much laughter, much life. Some of the people there are among the happiest, most blessed people I have ever met. I have come to believe, mostly from where I have lived and worked the past ten years that these promises of Jesus are only true for those who *choose* their lot, and not at all true for those who have poverty, imprisonment, thirst, persecution pressed upon them from the outside. I do not think poverty a good and desirable thing. Persecution creates terrible injustices. Those in my midst who are poor in all these ways are, for the most part, miserable, if their lot seems thrust upon them, outside of their control. Paradoxically, however, those in the midst of the community who have chosen to be poor, chosen to be persecuted, who have freely accepted the lot of the poor, casting their lot with them, often experience deep, abiding happiness and penetrating joy. The joy and blessedness promised by Jesus, at least in this life, comes to those who choose to identify with Jesus.

I have come to believe that we need to take the words of Jesus seriously, but in the context of his life. We often understand his words only as we see how he lived them out. For the Fundamentalist, Jesus' words can be dangerously death-dealing. For example: "Turn the other cheek" has been used for years to encourage women to

stay in abusive relationships. Jesus turned the other
cheek by confronting Pilate, saying, "Why do you strike
me if I speak the truth?" Jesus was not gentle in his cheek
turning. He did not fight back but neither did he just let
people walk all over him without challenging them to
confront their own behavior. All of Jesus' words regarding poverty and the poor demand the same nuancing.
Jesus chose to stand on the side of the poor and to look at
the world through their eyes. He experienced in his own
life their poverty. We need to be careful about glorifying
poverty, but we can stand on the side of the poor. So,
insightfully, the American Bishops' Pastoral Letter on the
Economy suggests that as Christian people our economic,
political and societal decisions, should be made in terms
of what they do *to, with, for* the economically poor. This
is what I am suggesting the gospel calls me, calls us all to.
We would cheapen the gospel if we were to maintain
that everyone should live in abject poverty. We capture
its wisdom when we recognize the challenge to stand in
solidarity with those who, sadly, do so live.

## A QUINTESSENTIAL DREAM

Since I am not striving to prove anything in this chapter, but only to raise the right questions, let me illustrate,
through a dream, another way of "feeling" our way into
this difficult subject of finding the face of Christ in the
poor. A woman whom I will call Irma told me some time
ago a very powerful dream. I have come to consider it
the prototypical middle-class American Catholic dream.
When she had this dream, Irma was in her late thirties,
married and the mother of three children. She and her
husband had been active in their suburban parish,
involved in liturgy, and adult education. They had been
to marriage encounter, had been among the first in their

area to experience the Cursillo, and were now making *The Spiritual Exercises of St. Ignatius in Everyday Life*. Irma explained that, for her, Mother Teresa had become an icon, an image, a symbol of God in her life. This dream occurred in the midst of her retreat. I share it in the first person as she told it.

My husband and I are in India, in a large rather dilapidated house, standing in the entrance hallway. We are talking to Mother Teresa, offering to come and serve with her for a number of years, if she will accept us. Mother Teresa smiles at us, a wonderful warm, accepting smile. She says that she would be most happy to have us come if we really want to, but our offering must be free, not driven by "shoulds" or "oughts" or guilt in any way. She invites us to go out for a walk in the city and decide if this is what we really want. As we spoke I was aware of the sound of what I was positive were many rats running around upstairs in the house. I could not see them, but I knew they were there.

My husband and I went out into the streets of Calcutta. It was not filled as we would have expected, with enormous crowds of people, some starving, lying on the streets, but rather the scene was extremely violent. It felt more like Beirut. Gun shots abounded, and people were beating on each other in every direction we looked. We were very frightened and we scurried, as others did, trying to avoid both the bullets and the beatings. We found ourselves around a corner, standing in the doorway to an exquisite French restaurant. We looked in the windows to discover about six or eight small tables, with elegant table cloths, napkins, wine goblets, several pieces of silverware, candles, a lovely ambience. I remember looking at the menu in the window and knowing that what I wanted to order cost $19.00. It seemed strange to be going into a French restaurant in the midst of Calcutta, while we were supposed to be deciding about coming to serve the dying poor of India, but we decided to go in. Entering, we discovered that everything that looked so pretty from the outside had been misleading. The wine goblets were cracked and dirty. The table-cloths and napkins were browning, dingy, the place was very tawdry, and, most amazing of all, there were rats scurrying around the floor, throughout the restaurant. The dream ended with that awareness of rats here too.

I am certain the meaning of the dream is clear but, just in case, let me comment on primary implications which were almost immediately clear to her. She felt (as I suspect many good, honest sincere American Christians of today regularly do) caught between the world with which she was familiar and something new, unfamiliar yet attractive. The world of abundance, fine foods, French restaurants, and all the things even relatively affluent Americans have previously taken for granted as the "good life," is being challenged by the call of a new world, a sense of mission, a concern for the poor, and an option in their behalf to which the gospel invites a response. Over the past ten or fifteen years our churches have consistently challenged us to be attentive to the poor, not to be simply caught up in getting and having more "stuff." We experience a growing desire to share what we have. Yet, fears abound about the unseen rats that exist in the world we have not yet fully entered.

We have also come to know the "rats" in the too comfortable world we have known, making it difficult to continue to be at home there now. The tablecloths are not as nice as they once were. Though God seems to beckon us into new ways of serving, of caring, of being with the poor, it is, indeed, an invitation. This style of life is not forced upon us. We are welcome to enter, but our entering must be free, without coercion. I do not want to totally solve that dream for you any more than I did for Irma, but I do invite you to stay with it. I would only add that I believe I do not know anyone who would have enjoyed the fine meal in a French restaurant any-more than Jesus! He loved to eat meals with friends, loved the companionship, but he could not feast very often because there were too many people who did not have any food at all.

This dream of Irma's has the "feeling" of what I sense so many of the best people I know today experience almost continuously. No longer at home "in the old dis-pensation," unsure where to move in the future, caught between two forces with "rats" everywhere. In terms of the premise of this book and this chapter, we have searched for and sometimes found God in many places, until, now, a new awareness of the message of the gospel suggests we need to look more broadly, more deeply, in places that we were not conscious of before. That con-sciousness can perhaps be best described, not as com-passion for the poor, but identity with the poor. The con-version going on in us these recent years flows directly from the fear and the deep good will we see in Irma's dream. It consists of a shift from helping others less for-tunate than ourselves to the awareness that we are among the unfortunates, and all of us together come before God as poor, broken, in need. Some people's bro-kenness is more apparent, but we all stand in need, together. Thus, to find God in the poor includes owning and seeking for God in the poverty that is our own.

## A SHIFT IN CONSCIOUSNESS

I can illustrate this shift in consciousness as it played itself out with our parish recently. For ten years St. Leo Parish operated with a mission statement, perhaps the first parish I know to have formulated one. Although the statement was in many ways excellent, two years ago we realized a need to change a number of its pieces. Some of the changes in our statement of mission resulted from the normal transitions within a parish, For example, we now had a number of small children, and the need for us to respond to family issues needed to be reflected in our mission in a way they had not required previously.

Some changes were more substantive, a shift in consciousness. We changed the prologue of our statement to reflect an emerging consciousness about ourselves and our identity as a parish. Originally the initial words asserted that: "St. Leo is a Catholic Christian Community of followers of Jesus of Nazareth, who believe that Jesus is central and decisive to our daily living...." Relying on some of the words of what has become a parish theme song, we changed this to read: "We assert that St. Leo is a Catholic Christian Community of Faith, *a Raggedy Band of Believers*...." We are a part of the messy army of those marching to the promised land, led by a child whose "holes in his hand match the holes in his shoes." We are not the scrubbed faces of film strips, but the real, live, wounded, broken, fragile body of Christ.

Previously our mission statement had declared that we were: "a Pastoral community, reaching out to others, in which everyone has a place, celebrating each person's uniqueness, especially embracing the poor, wounded and rejected." When we looked at this statement, almost unanimously the Pastoral Council now realized its paternalistic tone. We changed it to read "reaching out to each other, in which everyone has a place, especially embracing the poor, wounded and rejected *while acknowledging our own poverty, woundedness, and experience of rejection.*" Our mission was not just to others, but to ourselves. We are one with, not different from others. Finding the face of Christ in the poor means finding the face of Christ in the poverty that is in us. We can only come to Christ out of poverty. We may only learn that from contact with others who are more obviously poor than ourselves.

## RECOVERING CHRISTIANS

To say essentially the same thing in another way, I am not alone is realizing that the recent flourishing of twelve-step programs (Alcoholics Anonymous, Narcotics Anonymous, Alanon, Overeaters' Anonymous, Adult Children of Alcoholics, etc.) suggest that we are all Recovering Christians. (Have you heard about the new group for compulsive talkers, which I am told I should join? It's called, "On and on." There is another self-help group for compulsive over-achievers that has *thirty-six* steps.) In all seriousness we are all people who need to get over our compulsions and our addictions to be free of our slavery to patterns of behavior and the moral poverty that destroys us and others. We all need to acknowledge that we are powerless and need to rely on some power greater than ourselves. This is the beginning of healing for all of us. We all depend on a power greater than ourselves in whom we can do infinitely more than we can ask or imagine. We all need to make continual, fearless moral inventory of the people we have injured through our addictions. We need reconciliation, need to share that hurt we have done with at least one other human being so we will be able to acknowledge it to ourselves. We all need to move to the freedom of a twelfth step, wherein we reach back to help others caught in the same traps and addictions as ourselves. We act not from some position of moral superiority, but because we know our own recovery process depends on the offer of such help.

I am aware of the present critique of twelve-step programs that wonders whether, especially for some women, a healing process that starts with *powerlessness* is the best approach. That certainly needs to be considered. If our self-worth is already dangerously fragile perhaps, initially, some other entree is needed. But finally we are all a bit broken and, in general it seems helpful to acknowledge that. Finally, the church, the Raggedy Band of the followers of Jesus, is an enormous twelve-step program, caught in the cosmic struggle between what Gerald May calls "Grace and Addiction." The church at its best is the self-help group to *which everyone belongs, and from which no one may be excluded.*

One of the conversion points of my life during the past ten years frees me from the need, desire, or even belief that I need to be worthy to go to communion. The generation just ahead of me insisted, often, on confession before communion to get clean and ready to go. I believe now that we need to be rather messy to go to communion. As a people we come to eucharist not because we are good and deserve it, but because we need so desperately to be fed with a life not our own, to have a blood not our own flow through our veins with a power beyond our imaginings.

We reach this essential insight through the growing realization that we need to be with and work for and touch the lives of the poor for our own sake, not just for theirs, lest we forget our own poverty. We are all in the crowd outside the cathedral, pleading with those who search for God. We are all in need of their attention, their help and their love.

This is what makes the isolation of Americans, one from the other, so tragic, so critical. We are so able to isolate ourselves from the economically poor that we are unable to see or feel our identity with them. I sometimes tell my Republican relatives that if they were to stand for half-an-hour on the steps of my home they would no longer be able to vote as they do. If they saw the huddled crowds of homeless waiting for a warm meal, or the endless lines of women and children looking for a place to sleep, or the sick with no access to health care waiting outside our free clinic in the rain, they would be touched. Politics aside, many Americans do not ever have to see or rub shoulders with the poor. They have no access to the stories of the twenty percent of our people who are simply not "making it." They do not know of the millions in even more tragic condition throughout the world, and this ignorance impoverishes us all.

I once drove two of my relatives around my neighborhood. About 8:30 P.M. there were three women on a street corner, dressed in very short skirts, looking at passing cars. The woman I was with asked what those women were doing. I realized she had never seen a prostitute, at least of the street-walking variety before. She was able to imagine they all looked like Julia Roberts and were likely to find some Richard Gere who would one day rescue them from a lucrative, if temporary life. When we are unaware of the visible, physical, tangible wounds on a high percentage of the body of Christ, we tend to deny our own less visible wounds, and live in a world of massive pretense.

### LESSONS LEARNED FROM THE POOR

Let me share some things that I feel graced about in my life, things from which I have learned, or at least am learning by living and working among the poor.

#### Some lessons only the poor can teach

In the summer of 1992 I had another illuminating experience at the moment of a death and funeral. Ray was not a member of the precisely economically poor, but he was a charter member of a disenfranchised segment of our complicated world—the gay community. Ray committed suicide, gassing himself in his car. Friends of his, not knowing where else to turn, came to our parish and asked us to help with his funeral arrangements. They explained that Ray had been brought up a Catholic, his aunt was a nun, and he had been an altar boy in Chicago many years before. In my absence one of our staff assured the friends that we would be pleased to help them bury Ray. When I finally met with the friends I discovered that Ray had a stage name, Christi Rae, and was the foremost female impersonator in the northwestern United States. Because he was well known from Vancouver, B.C. to Portland, Oregon, Ray's funeral was massive. Six hundred people crowded into our church to sing, to pray, and to tell stories of Ray's bizarre, tragic, but amazingly fruitful life. The congregation was predominantly gay and lesbian, many coming as couples, many in drag, all weeping, touched by the death of someone they loved, and whom they knew loved them. I found myself deeply moved by the stories, yet frankly confused by dimensions of Christi Rae's life that I do not easily comprehend.

Ray's brother, whom he had not seen for fifteen years, came from Chicago. After the funeral I talked to him. I knew he had never reconciled himself either to his brother's sexual orientation or his life-style. I said to him, "This must be difficult for you." His reply overwhelmed me and has stayed with me ever since. "Yes, it was difficult, but also terribly important. I never understood my brother. In fact, I closed my eyes to his existence. I realize that if I died tomorrow, perhaps fifty people would attend the funeral, and two or three would really care at all. My brother, whom I had neglected, looked down on and discounted, had an enormous community of people that loved him, whose lives he touched, and for whom his death is truly tragic. He had a community beyond my imagining. *I need to understand this.*"

When we do not see how others live, we cannot understand them, and we thus judge and criticize. We make them separate from ourselves, and both they and we are impoverished by that blindness. When we open ourselves to the experiences of those who seem to us poor, we are able, like Ray's brother, to experience our own poverty. My point in all of this is simply that we learn about Christ, we discover something of God, and we learn about ourselves from the poor, and those who are close to them.

### People not projects are central

One of my favorite people in and around St. Leo is Galen. Galen, in his mid-thirties, suffers from a form of autism. Ten years ago Galen was all but totally incommunicative. He talked only to his own hand, in various voices from several characters inside his head. He smoked incessantly, coughed, and sometimes yelled at his shaking right hand. He never entered into contact with anyone else. For the past several years Galen has lived with a family in the parish, almost as another child with their natural three. Galen has changed dramatically. Though still not "normal" perhaps, he does interact with and sometimes delight others.

Galen spends a large amount of his free time in our parish offices, just hanging around, drinking coffee, going through donated clothes looking for skirts for his sister (who does not need them). Often Galen comes into my office through a door left slightly ajar. Always he comes when I am doing something I consider important. He comes, as a veiled presence of Jesus, quietly demanding attention. In almost every instance I have to force myself to stop what I am doing and pay attention to him. Sometimes I succeed, sometimes I do not. But always at times most inconvenient he is there. He often enters and looks at the pictures on a bulletin board behind my desk. He loves to look at my ordination picture showing a much younger, much thinner, very different looking person. Galen gazes for long minutes at this picture, then back at me, then at the picture again. Invariably, he eventually asks me: "Who is that?" With equal consistency I say: "That's me, twenty-five years ago." Again he looks at me, at the picture, at me again, in simple silence, until he finally breaks out into a gigantic grin, laughing at me, and inviting me to laugh at myself. Galen truly brings the presence of Christ into my office. He forces me to be less task and more people oriented, teasing me, playing with me, delighting me if I take the time to allow him to do so.

Before I arrived at St. Leo in 1984, the parish had become a Sanctuary Church, harboring a heroic family from El Salvador. The parents of this family, with only three or four grades of education, are nonetheless poets and philosophers. I speak no Spanish. Their English, better now, was very labored in my early years with them. Still, they had so much to say, words of profound, pain-induced wisdom. I am instinctively a very abrupt person; I rush from one thing to another, often talking over my shoulder as I go by. With this family I had to force myself to stop, to listen, to hear them, to talk slowly, clearly so they could understand me. Also they are very short, and when I spoke with them I often felt like I was, literally, talking down to them, so I had to learn to stop, to sit, to notice, to speak to them face-to-face. I need to do the same to truly communicate with almost everyone I contact, but this family taught me that lesson most profoundly.

## The Poor have no choice but to trust

I learned a lot of trust from Gary, a Jesuit friend with whom I lived for years. At the time, Gary directed a drop-in center for street people downtown. Here he worked in the midst of the truly poor where the face of Christ was the bruised, beaten, crucified face. Nativity House ran on a slim shoe-string, but always managed to survive. People brought food, or they scrounged for what they needed through other agencies, rarely buying anything. Gary prided himself on never buying coffee. Whenever they got short someone would magically show up with more. They brewed ten to fifteen pots a day. One winter the supply was very low, only enough for a first morning pot. Gary gave in and went out to buy just five pounds. Twenty minutes later he returned to discover that someone had brought into Nativity House one hundred pounds of premium (Starbucks) coffee. Gary was totally embarrassed, more before God than anyone, and he never bought coffee again. It would come when it was supposed to be there, and he had to live with the not knowing.

Those who work with the poor learn to trust in ways often unimaginable to others. People often ask where they get the food to feed over five hundred people a day in the Hospitality Kitchen located in our parish's former school building. The people who serve in the kitchen respond honestly that they do not know. They get what they need to have each day. God gives them, this day, their daily "bread," and the meals are far more than bread, always substantial, balanced, plentiful. Whatever is required shows up when needed.

### The Poor have perspective

I have learned from other friends who work directly with the poor how to laugh. I have learned anew that life "is too important to be taken seriously." I have come to believe that the happiest people I know are those who have cast their lot with the economically disadvantaged. Somehow they are able to relativize their problems, all relatively minor next to the struggle to simply survive. I know no human being who laughs more easily nor more deeply than Bix, my Jesuit priest friend who has lived in the midst of the poor for thirty years. His laugh infects all who work with or around him. The problems and struggles he faces and enters into each day are far from funny, but somehow provide a prism through which he is able to see the hilarity of everything else.

### Remember the Mystery

A Native American woman in our parish, who runs a drop-in center for Native Americans on the streets had taught me a reverence for the mystery of life. At times Joanne helps us pray in her native fashion. Dressed luxuriously in native clothes, carrying her sacred Eagle Feather, she comes before us inviting us into a silence which usually lasts far beyond our comfort. She forces us to stillness, to reverence for the earth and the water and for all the elements before us. She comes from a tradition so different from my own, from a people whom we have made poor (not just materially, but by our failure to appreciate their gifts), but I have felt her reduce an entire congregation to respectful, reverential silence and honest deep prayer.

## Celebrate Life

I have learned how to celebrate from the people of L'Arche, those with handicapping conditions who are so central to our parish community. Previously I spoke of Bill, who led a sophisticated cynical doctor to a simple faith. Bill often leads us in prayer, in dance, in celebration. I remember most vividly a Holy Spirit mass some years ago. I think this constitutes the liturgical highlight of my life. St. Leo Parish community begins our year together, as many schools do, with a renewal of Spirit early in September. We re-create the Spirit of Pentecost as best we can. This liturgy has become one of our major celebrations. This particular Spirit mass ended with a small parade. A woman dressed as a clown came into the church after communion. To the melody of our parish theme song about the Raggedy Band, she wandered through the church inviting children (and others brave enough) to join her. She passed out little kazoos, and drums and bells and bottles to bang on. About thirty children joined in her parade. Bill also joined in, bringing up the rear of the parade as it wove throughout the community. The clown had timed her march to have the children come to lay down their instruments before the altar as the final verse ended; then they would disperse back to their places. All went well, except that Bill was not yet done parading. All the others had laid down their instruments and returned to their places, but as we sang the final words, Bill did one more trip down the center aisle, grin-

ning from ear to ear, ringing his bell and dancing. We
sang:

And did you know, that the lead child walking
doesn't want to go,
And can you see, where Broadway turns into Calvary,
Boom ticka, ticka, ticka, boom ticka, ticka, ticka, boom
ticka, ticka ticka boom.

Bill returned to the altar alone, gently laid down his
bell at the altar as the last note sounded. He turned
solemnly to the congregation and with impeccable tim-
ing, bowed. We applauded. He bowed again, and then
again. One of the L'Arche assistants was just getting out
of her pew to come and retrieve Bill, but he knew his
moment was over and went to the foot of the altar plat-
form, turned, and bowed his head to await the final
prayer which he knew to be next.

Several minutes later, still through my tears I prayed
the final prayer for God's spirit, but already the Spirit
was in our midst. Bill, unfettered by the customs or conditions that bind the rest of us had unleashed that Spirit
in us and I thank God we had sense enough not to ham-
per him. We were led to God by the apparently weakest
among us.

*Working from the Ashes*

Again all of us are poor and we need to discover that. I
have been reading lately some of the growing body of
"Men's Literature," trying to discover what it means
today to be a man. The book I liked least was Robert
Bly's *Iron John*. I did, however, love one section that
spoke eloquently of men's fragility. The King's son had
to go back and work in the basement of another castle,

needed to be reduced to working among the ashes. He and we cannot truly become the Kings' sons that we indeed are without at some time being reduced to *ashes*.

Men find it so difficult to ask for help, to acknowledge that we are weak, or poor. So often in pastoral work I find men unable to admit that their marriage is falling apart, or that they have lost contact with their son or daughter, or no longer had competence in their job, until it is too late. In myself and every man I know there is a scared five-year-old that never goes away, but to whom we give scant attention. Men in our society desperately need to get in touch with the ashes. We need that just so that others can get along with us, not to mention so that we can be saved by Jesus! Often men are unable to enter into any contact with God because of this same inability to acknowledge any need, any dependence on a power greater than themselves.

Certainly when we talk about finding God in the poor, we need to look at the truly, economically poor. We do this partially because they help us to see the poverty in ourselves. It is critical to acknowledge the reality that we are all poor; we are not all we would like to be in our jobs, in our homes, as husbands or wives, as parents. We are not all that we would like to be in our desire to transform the world. This entire chapter simply maintains that we need to have some regular, in-depth contact with the poor, with the face of Christ where he said he would be found, if only to discover the face of the poor in ourselves. Then out of our need we can turn to God, to Christ who comes not to the healthy but to the sick.

## CONCLUSION

I have shared many stories of St. Leo that are uplifting, life-giving, even in the midst of pain. Not all my experiences are so affirmative. The most difficult individual for me in our community is a somewhat cunning, mildly mentally-ill person whom we call "Nazi Bob." He earned that nickname by goose-stepping into church on occasion, and in days before I arrived, frequently saluting people with a "Heil Hitler."

Bob is very difficult to be around. He knows especially how to push my buttons. We ask people not to panhandle around the church, especially as people are coming to, or leaving worship, but Bob, who does not need to panhandle, always does. We ask him to treat our staff and our buildings with respect, but Bob often curses staff people, sometimes throws coffee on the walls, and generally has no single ounce of respect in him. I rarely get angry, but I become enraged at Bob about twice a week. I banish him from the property, but he returns in a few days, acting as if nothing has happened. He appears astounded when I remind him that I told him to leave and never come back. How could I do that to innocent him? Bob never goes away, and he never seems to change. He is perhaps put here to free me from whatever "time in purgatory" might mean today. I do not like Bob. I certainly, despite all pious disclaimers, do not love him. But I need him. Without Bob's presence I could begin to think I have arrived at some spiritual plateau. He constantly reminds me how far I have to go, how much the same I still am, and how distant is the game I talk from the one I play. In Jungian terms, Bob provides for me a shadow character. He is so much like me in his obstinacy, in his refusal to understand what he does not like, in his rebelliousness. My rage against him forces me to look more carefully at myself. I need the poor, and I need Bob.

I have been helped to understand myself by our Jesuit self-understanding. In a recent General Congregation, in an atypical fit of humility, the Jesuits said about ourselves that:

"A Jesuit is a sinner, loved by God."

I like that. I can live with, live within that realistic description. We begin to define ourselves by the reality of our poverty, our sinfulness. Were we to remain only with that part of our definition, we would be false to the glory of our call. But we are not just sinners. Like everyone else, we are loved and called, chosen and redeemed sinners. There are no other kinds of people, only poor people who are saved anyway, because of the love God shows for us in Jesus. This description of a Jesuit is exactly duplicated in every living, breathing human being. We are all sinners loved by God. We all need to find God's face among the poor, within the poverty that is ours, in order to recognize the fact.

As I began this book and each chapter of it by prayer, let me end by inviting the reader into a final prayerful experience. Take a minute to read slowly this selection from Mark's gospel:

When Jesus returned to Capernaum after some days, it became known that he was at home. Many gathered together so that there was no longer room for them, not even around the door, and he preached the word to them. They came bringing to him a paralytic, carried by four men. Unable to get near Jesus because of the crowd, they opened up the roof above him. After they had broken through, they let down the mat on which the paralytic was lying. When Jesus saw their faith, he said to the paralytic, "Child, your sins are forgiven." Now some of the scribes were sitting there asking themselves,

"Why does this man speak that way? He is blas-
pheming. Who but God alone can forgive sins?"
Jesus immediately knew in his mind what they
were thinking to themselves, so he said, "Why are
you thinking such things in your hearts? Which is
easier, to say to the paralytic, 'Your sins are forgiv-
en,' or to say 'Rise, pick up your mat and walk?' But
that you may know that the Son of Man has authority to forgive sins on earth"...he said to the paralytic,
"I say to you, rise, pick up your mat and go home."
He rose, picked up his mat at once, and went away
in the sight of everyone (Mk 2:1–12).

As in a previous gospel passage I invite you not just to
think about this healing miracle but to enter into it. Take
a moment to imagine yourself, lying on the mat, paralyzed. All of us are that paralytic; each of us is unable to
move, to love, to act in ways we want to. Our poverty is
in this paralysis. Be still enough on the mat to know
where, how, why you are paralyzed. Know what it is you
would like Jesus to heal. Perhaps it helps to name for
yourself who the people would be who would bring you
before Jesus when you are not able to get to him on your
own. Who are the friends who have carried you here?

As you lie on the mat, imagine Jesus looking down at
you with enormous love. Let him say to you, over and
over until you begin to believe it, "Get up and walk; you
do not need to be paralyzed in the same way any more.
Get up and walk; get up and walk; get up and walk."

Finding God, finding the face of Jesus in the poor
begins with discerning the loving, healing face of Jesus
in my own poverty, my own paralysis. Seek for God
where God may be found.

# Postscript

## Finding God in the Natural World

*Praise the Lord from the earth,*
*you sea monsters and all depths;*
*Fire and hail, snow and mist,*
*storm winds that fulfill his word;*
*You mountains and all you hills,*
*you fruit trees and all you cedars;*
*You wild beasts and all tame animals,*
*you creeping things and you winged fowl*
(Ps 148:7–10).

*We know that all creation is groaning in labor*
*pains even until now* (Ro 8:22).

I offer a postscript because I am embarrassed not to have enough to say to make a chapter out of the topic of finding God in the natural world. I come from a tradition that has focused too centrally on human, interpersonal relations, focused on the human person as central to creation, and as the locus of God's presence. In *The Spiritual Exercises*, St. Ignatius considered all created things other than the individual retreatant as existing for our benefit, to be used insofar as they help us to our God-directed end, and not to be used insofar as they hinder this purpose. In other words, the things of the world exist for us, with little value in their own right. We have a "dominion over," not a "coexistence with" this world we inhabit. Lately, under the influence of an entire body of writing from Al Gore to Thomas Berry suggesting an ecological reverence for the earth, I experience a deep, critical need to apologize for this historic oversight, this critical misdirection in Ignatian and most other Christian spirituality. I want to suggest before I close, that we can and must discover and reverence God abundantly in the world around us. We must learn to be as concerned with biocide or geocide as we are with homicide and genocide.

In addition to the areas of consideration in the previous chapters detailing the ways I have discovered God in the past, for the future I must encourage myself and others towards the possibility, even the necessity of finding God in the Natural World.

## FROM OUR CATHOLIC TRADITION

Indeed, I discover grounds for this reverence within the best of my Catholic and my Ignatian traditions. Though the Catholic Church often neglects its earthy side, its own pervasive materialism, still our very sacramental character reminds us that we have always used the stuff of the earth to help us find God. We have always said, if not appreciated, that water, oil, bread, wine, incense, candles, fire, musical chords, art, poetry, statues, signs and symbols of all kinds lead us into contact with an immanent God. We enter into the Christian community by plunging into the waters, and being raised from the tomb-womb of death to new life. We remember the presence of Jesus in our midst by taking bread, tearing it as was torn the body of Jesus, and distributing that torn body-bread to all. We usher in the time of resurrection by lighting an extravagant bonfire against the darkness of night. Later in the same service, we open up the waters of new birth in Christ by that earthiest sign of all, the plunging of a phallic candle into the water's womb so it becomes fecund, pregnant with new life for the catechumens and children who will enter it.

In many ways, in the heart of our tradition, lies a deep reverence for the things of earth, this created world and the matter of our universe. But we have lost touch with that natural world so fully, so easily. We have replaced the pool of baptism with a few dabs of water from a bowl, have refrained from bread for more convenient wafers, and have too often let our Easter fire consist of a handful of sticks, quickly lit, then left. We have not stood around that fire to tell our ancient, earthy stories. The foundation for a more ecological, earth-based spirituality already exists in germ and invites a recovery of our finest traditions.

### FROM THE IGNATIAN TRADITION

The Jesuit Poet, Gerard Manley Hopkins, overwhelms his reader with the imagery of the earth, his excitement about fireflies, and finches wings, about "weeds in wheel rushes," about "rose moles all in stipple upon trout that swim." Hopkins' awe toward God is not confined by any means to the merely human, for God "veins violets and small trees makes, more and more." God is enmeshed in Hopkins' spiritual, natural world, and we can find "the dearest freshness deep down (in) things."

Fr. Tom Clarke, S.J., in a recent dialogue with Thomas Berry (*Befriending the Earth*, Twenty-Third Publications, 1991), points out that Ignatius himself celebrates the presence of God in creation profoundly in the final exercise of *The Spiritual Exercises*, the Contemplation for Obtaining Love. In a kind of ecological pre-history, Ignatius speaks of the various levels of creation, inviting the retreatant to discover and celebrate God in each of them. We prayerfully rejoice in God's gift of creation, God giving the very self of God within that creation (especially in Jesus), God laboring in that creation on our behalf, and finally God transforming that creation. In some ways, as Clarke points out, Ignatius asserts forcibly that we do not have to leave the world of creation to find God.

We celebrate this discovery of God in the natural world in another Jesuit, Teilhard de Chardin, poet, theologian, paleontologist, who celebrates the Universe. Indeed he writes about "The Mass of the World," in which he consecrates the entire created world into Christ's body. His entire body of work wondrously expands Paul's hint that the world and everything in it, human, animal, mineral, and vegetable, groans, struggles, and vibrates in one enormous act of giving birth to Christ. The hymn the psalmist sings to God, through the voices of the natural world is not an unknown strain in the immanent spirituality I have suggested in the previous pages.

## PERSONAL CHALLENGE

Still, I recognize my own poverty in developing this awareness of God's presence. I can tell story after story of my own discovery of God's intimate connection with my life through reflective awareness of all my human experiences, in moments of communal worship, in the effort to identify with the poor, and the poverty within myself. I wish I could share the same kinds of stories about how I have been touched by, amazed at, the power, beauty, and love of God within the world we inhabit. This presence exists not just to be used by us, nor just to be appreciated, but as the presence of God in its own right, and for its own sake.

I can recall one precious moment of such an awareness, as I stood beneath the splashing waters of Victoria Falls, on the border between Zambia and Zimbabwe. As far as the eye could see waters poured into the surging Zambezi. The sheer volume overwhelmed me; I remember thinking instantaneously: "This water flows whether or not I see it! This power is present, this grand beauty every moment of every day, with only an occasional witness." I wish the same reverence for rocks, and snakes, and grains of sand. Our species' survival demands such reverence for rain forests, top soil, spotted owls, sea life, oil reserves, the rays of the sun, the entire mystery of creation.

In each chapter of this book I have suggested some meditative process for the reader to touch the mystery of God in everyday experience. Though my personal reflective awareness of the God completely enmeshed in creation may be slight, I encourage you to touch your own. Before closing this book, as a bridge into a spirituality needed for our future, I encourage you to remember as vividly as you can some precious moment of God's revelation to you in nature. Recall a waterfall, a sunset, an ocean wave, a mountain top that brought you at least momentarily into the presence of God. Where has God been present to you in nature?

I am ashamed that I neglect this ever more significant manifestation of God's presence. As I have written to encourage attentive awareness of God in every fiber of our lives, I know that the future challenges me to grow in this creation awareness. As I leave these reflections, I can only encourage you to join me in this expanded sensibility toward a world "charged with the grandeur of God."